Teachers, Human Rights and Diversity:
educating citizens in multicultural societies

Teachers, Human Rights and Diversity:
educating citizens in multicultural societies

edited by Audrey Osler

Trentham Books

Stoke on Trent, UK and Sterling, USA

Trentham Books Limited
Westview House   22883 Quicksilver Drive
734 London Road   Sterling
Oakhill   VA 20166-2012
Stoke on Trent   USA
Staffordshire
England ST4 5NP

First published 2005. Reprinted 2007, 2008.

British Library Cataloguing-in-Publication Data
A catalogue record for this book is available from the British
Library

ISBN-13: 978-1-85856-339-8

*Cover photographs: Students at Villiers High School in London
in their play, Migrating Swallows. This was performed at the
international school conference on world issues organised by
Villiers students in October 2004.*

*We thank Dai Jones and Villiers High School for permission to
reproduce the photographs.*

Designed and typeset by Trentham Print Design Ltd., Chester
and printed in Great Britain by Cpod, Wiltshire.

Contents

Foreword

James A. Banks

The quests for rights by ethnic minority groups that intensified in the 1960s and 1970s, the increase in international migration, the tightening of national borders, and the growth in the number of nation-states make the issues examined in this book significant and timely. The number of recognised nation-states increased from 43 in 1900 to approximately 190 in 2000. The number of people living outside their country of birth or citizenship grew from 120 million in 1990 to 160 million in 2000 (Martin and Widgren, 2002). The growth in international migration, the increasing recognition of structural inequality within democratic nation-states, and the growing recognition and legitimacy of international human rights have problematised issues related to citizenship and citizenship education in nation-states throughout the world, and especially in the Western democracies.

The chapters in this book examine some of the intractable problems and issues that schools in democratic nation-states experience when they try to help students become effective citizens within schools and societies that are stratified by race and social class and that practice religious separatism. The case studies in this book are from England, Northern Ireland, the Republic of Ireland, and the United States. However, the insights and findings in them have important implications for all democratic societies in which an important aim of the schools is to help students become democratic citizens who have a commitment to social justice, human rights, and civic action.

The authors make it clear that teachers and schools must practice democracy and human rights in order for these ideals to be internalised by students. Schools and classrooms must become microcosms and exemplars of democracy and social justice in order for students to develop democratic attitudes and learn how to practice democracy. As Dewey stated, 'all genuine education comes through experience' (1959: 13). Several of the chapters in this book describe examples of teachers and teacher educators that exemplify democratic teaching and student learning that should be helpful to school practitioners and teacher educators. Other chapters report encouraging empirical findings which indicate that a democratic curriculum has positive effects on student attitudes toward outgroup members. However, as this volume makes explicit, much work must be done before most teachers and schools in democratic multicultural nation-states actualise democracy and social justice in their curricula, teaching materials, and in their attitudes, expectations, and behaviours.

Multicultural democratic nation-states must find ways to help students develop balanced and thoughtful attachments and identifications with their cultural community, their nation-state, and with the global community. In some cases, such as in the European Union and in parts of Asia, it is also important for citizens to develop a regional identification. This book – as well as an increasingly rich literature on diversity and citizenship education within a global context (Banks, 2004a; Gutmann, 2003; Kymlicka, 1995; Nussbaum, 1996; Suàrez-Orozco and Qin-Hilliard, 2004) – describes how nation-states have generally failed to help students develop a delicate balance of identifications. Rather, they have given priority to national identifications and have neglected the community cultures of students as well as the knowledge and skills students need to function in an interdependent global world.

Nationalists in nation-states throughout the world worry that if they help students develop identifications and attachments to their cultural communities they will not acquire sufficiently strong attachments to their nation-states. Kymlicka argues that nationalists have a 'zero-sum conception of identity (2004: xiv). Nussbaum (1996) worries that a focus on nationalism will prevent students from developing a commitment to cosmopolitan values such as human rights and social justice, values which transcend national boundaries, cultures, and times.

As this volume makes explicit, identity is multiple, changing, overlapping and contextual, rather than fixed and static. The multicultural conception of identity – which is supported by the analyses and findings in this book – is that citizens who have clarified and thoughtful attachments to their community cultures, languages and values are more likely than citizens who are stripped of their cultural attachments to develop reflective identifications with their nation-state (Banks, 2004b; Kymlicka, 2004). They will also be better able to function as effective citizens in the global community. Nation-states, however, must make structural changes that reduce structural inequality and that legitimise and give voice to the hopes, dreams and visions of their marginalised citizens in order for them to develop strong and clarified commitments to the nation-states and its goals.

To effectively educate cosmopolitan and democratic citizens in ways envisioned by the authors of this book, nation-states must also balance unity and diversity, an important theme that Osler sets forth in the opening chapter of this book. Citizens in a diverse democratic society should be able to maintain attachments to their cultural communities as well as participate in the shared national culture. Unity without diversity results in cultural repression and hegemony. Diversity without unity leads to Balkanisation and the fracturing of the nation-state. Diversity and unity should co-exist in a delicate balance in democratic multicultural nation-states. A balance between diversity and unity is needed because their relationship is an ongoing, complex, and dynamic process and an ideal that is never fully attained.

As the chapters in this book indicate, it is essential for both mainstream groups and groups on the margins of society to participate in the formulation and implementation of societal goals related to diversity, unity, human rights, and citizenship if democracy is to prevail. This will happen only if dominant and marginalised groups share power and participate in decision-making with equal status. Both groups must also participate in cooperative action in order to advance democracy and social justice within the nation-state.

Deliberation and the sharing of power by mainstream and marginalised groups are essential for the construction and per-petuation of a just, moral, and participatory democratic nation-state in a culturally diverse society. The authors of this infor-mative, visionary and practical book advance both theory and practice about ways in which schools can educate cosmo-politan citizens who are able and willing to act to make their communities, nations, and the world caring and humane places in which to live.

References

Banks, J. A. (Ed.) (2004a) *Diversity and Citizenship Education: global perspectives.* San Francisco: Jossey-Bass.

Banks, J. A. (2004b) Teaching for social justice, diversity, and citizenship in a global age, *The Educational Forum*, 68: 297-305.

Dewey, J. (1959) *Experience and Education.* New York: Macmillan.

Gutmann, A. (2003) *Identity in Democracy.* Princeton, NJ: Princeton University Press.

Kymlicka, W. (1995) *Multicultural Citizenship: a liberal theory of minority rights.* New York: Oxford University Press.

Kymlicka, W. (2004) *Foreword.* In J. A. Banks (Ed.) *Diversity and Citizenship Education: global perspectives* (pp. xiii-xviii). San Francisco: Jossey-Bass.

Martin, P. and Widgren, J. (2002) International migration: facing the challenge. *Population Reference Bulletin*, 57, No. 1. Washington, DC: Population Reference Bureau.

Nussbaum, M. C. (1996) J. Cohen (Ed.) *For Love of Country?* Boston: Beacon Press.

Suárez-Orozco, M. M. and Qin-Hilliard, D. B. (Eds.) (2004) *Globalisation, Culture and Education in the New Millennium.* Berkeley: University of California Press.

Acknowledgements

I would like to thank a number of people who have supported and encouraged me during the preparation of this book.

Professor James A. Banks, Director of the Center for Multicultural Education at the University of Washington who convened the International Consensus Panel on Education for Global Citizenship in Contexts of Diversity and fellow members of the panel: Cherry A. McGee Banks, Carlos E. Cortes, Carole Hahn, Merry Merryfield, Kogilia Moodley, Stephen Murphy-Shigematsu, Mark Purcell, Walter C. Parker and Farhat J. Ziadeh. Our discussions and debates have led me to think more deeply about education for democratic citizenship in contexts of diversity.

Professor Mab Huang of Soochow University, Taipei, and fellow human rights activists and colleagues whose work to ensure that human rights education became part of the school curriculum in Taiwan is an inspiration.

Eno Nakamura, Akane Yoshino and development education workers, volunteers and members of DEAR, Japan, who enabled me to spend several enriching weeks in Japan during 2003 exchanging ideas and experiences of children's rights and cosmopolitan citizenship.

Colleagues at the Centre for Citizenship Studies in Education at the University of Leicester. Hugh Starkey, whose collaboration in *Changing Citizenship* and other concurrent projects has enriched my thinking. Special thanks to Barbara Hall for her work in liaising with contributors and for ensuring this book progressed as I prepared to take up a new post at the University of Leeds.

Colleagues at the Centre for Citizenship and Human Rights Education at the University of Leeds. Katie Allen and Julie Hastings both assisted in preparing the typescript.

Acronyms and abbreviations

ABC   anti-bias curriculum
ACT   All Children Together
BBC   British Broadcasting Corporation
BORIS   Bill of Rights in Schools
CCEA   Council for the Curriculum Examinations and Assessment
CDU   Curriculum Development Unit
CRC   Community Relations Council
CRE   Commission for Racial Equality
CSPE   Civic Social and Political Education
DEAR   Development Education Association and Resource Centre of Japan
DEFY   Development Education for Youth
DES   Department of Education and Science
DENI   Department of Education for Northern Ireland
DfES   Department for Education and Skills
DICE   Development and Intercultural Education
ECHR   European Convention for the Protection of Human Rights and Fundamental Freedoms
EMU   Education for Mutual Understanding
ERO   Educational Reform (Northern Ireland) Order
EU   European Union
GCSE   General Certificate of Secondary Education
HRC   Human Rights Commission
HRE   Human Rights Education
ICAR   Information Centre on Asylum and Refugees
IEA   International Association for the Evaluation of Educational Achievement
INTO   Irish National Teachers' Organisation

KS2	Key Stage 2
LEA	Local Education Authority
MP	Member of Parliament
NASS	National Asylum Support Service
NCCA	National Council for Curriculum and Assessment
NCCRI	National Consultative Committee on Racism and Interculturalism
NGO	non-governmental organisation
NI	Northern Ireland
NICIE	Northern Ireland Council for Integrated Education
NIHRC	Northern Ireland Human Rights Commission
NPAR	National Plan Against Racism
PGCE	Post Graduate Certificate in Education
PSHE	Personal Social and Health Education
QCA	Qualifications and Curriculum Authority
RE	Religious Education
RRAA	Race Relations (Amendment) Act 2000
SEN	Special Educational Needs
SLSS	Second Level Support Service
SPHE	Social Personal and Health Education
SVP	Society of Saint Vincent de Paul
TSN	Targeting Social Need
TTA	Teacher Training Agency
TY	Transition Year
UDHR	Universal Declaration of Human Rights
UN	United Nations

Preface

Audrey Osler

n June 2003, UNESCO's International Institute for Educational Planning (IIEP) in Paris hosted an invitation seminar to examine some of the challenges faced by planners and policy-makers concerned with the education of young people within our globalised world and increasingly diverse local communities and schools. The same year, the Center for Multicultural Education at the University of Washington, Seattle, brought together scholars to form an International Consensus Panel on Education for Global Citizenship in Contexts of Diversity and to consider how schools in multicultural democracies might best educate young people for citizenship. Members of the panel, drawn from Canada, the United States, Japan and Britain, debated the key principles and concepts that need to be included in educating for citizenship in multicultural and democratic nation states. These two independent initiatives brought together researchers and others responsible for policy development in schools, teacher education and other settings from different countries and regions and both produced publications to inform and support educators and administrators in a range of countries (see IIEP, 2005 and Banks *et al.*, 2005).

Although ambitious in scope, the IIEP and the University of Washington initiatives are not exceptional in the sense that they reflect a broader and growing interest across the world in how educators can prepare young citizens to participate in contexts of diversity. Other parallel debates are occurring at regional and national levels, as politicians, policy-makers, teachers and researchers promote and develop education programmes for citizenship and human rights. For example, at a symposium on education for sustainable development held at Rikkyo University in Tokyo in August 2003, participants from across the Asia Pacific region engaged in a thoughtful and lively debate about citizenship and identity and whether it is useful to promote and develop a regional identity alongside specific national identities. In February 2004 educators and politicians in Macedonia held a national conference on citizenship education, with support from the British Association for Central and Eastern Europe. At this event there was lively and sometimes heated debate among participants, who were drawn from the ethnic Albanian and ethnic Macedonian populations, about questions of diversity and equality and about ways forward for citizenship education in the post-conflict context.

In Taiwan, a group of educators from Soochow University and Taipei Teachers' College hosted a number of conferences in April 2004 to publicise local and international initiatives in human rights education (HRE). Their intention was to gain the support of school principals and politicians in implementing HRE as a newly recognised subject in the Taiwanese school curriculum. In South Africa HRE is a formally agreed element of the school curriculum, but since it is not yet a standard part of teacher education it has not become a genuine entitlement for all South African children. From 2003 to 2005, colleagues the University of Western Cape, supported by the British Council higher education link programme, are engaged in research into children's understandings of human rights so that these can inform the teacher education programme.

I have been privileged to participate in each of the initiatives outlined above and to learn from colleagues working in very different contexts but with the same overall purpose, namely to educate young people for citizenship and democracy in contexts of diversity. At the beginning of the 21st century the concept of citizenship is changing. The lives of ordinary citizens are influenced not only by what happens in their local communities and at a national level but also by developments at regional and global levels. The projects I have highlighted above are educational responses to processes of globalisation and democratisation.

Human rights, cosmopolitan citizenship and education

For democracy to flourish, regional (for example, European) and international institutions need to develop in more democratic and accountable ways. A number of academics, most notably David Held (1995 and 1996), have developed the concept of 'cosmopolitan democracy' to envisage a new locus for democracy. He argues for the building of human rights into the constitution of states and for the creation and development of regional and global institutions which would co-exist alongside states but over-ride them on issues which escape their control, such as monetary management, environmental issues, elements of security and new forms of communication. In fact, many such developments and reforms have been introduced since the mid-1990s: for example, the South African constitution is based explicitly on human rights; in the UK constitutional reform in the form of the Human Rights Act 1998 has incorporated the European Convention on Human Rights (ECHR) into domestic law. Already at international and regional levels:

> From the UN system to the EU, from changes to the law of war to the entrenchment of human rights, from the emergence of international environmental regimes to the foundation of the International Criminal Court, there is also another narrative being told – the narrative which seeks to reframe human activity and entrench it in law, rights and responsibilities. (Held, 2001)

A cosmopolitan democracy implies cosmopolitan citizenship. Cosmopolitan citizenship requires a cosmopolitan and humanistic vision. Such a vision underpins the Charter of the United Nations (UN) 1945, based on human rights, justice and equality. In a globalised world individuals are likely to have multiple identities and multiple loyalties. The cosmopolitan vision needs to recognise and embrace diversity within as well as between communities.

A cosmopolitan vision and the skills to participate in contexts of diversity are not innate. They need to be fostered and taught. In other words, there needs to be education for cosmopolitan citizenship based on human rights, to enable citizens to help shape our common future through action and participation at all levels, from the local to the global. I have explored the rationale and key elements of education for cosmopolitan citizenship in more detail elsewhere (Osler and Vincent, 2002; Osler, 2005; Osler and Starkey, 2005).

Teachers, Human Rights and Diversity: educating citizens in multicultural societies is intended as a contribution to on-going debates about effective ways of teaching and learning for cosmopolitan citizenship. It examines some of the conditions in which schools are working to introduce citizenship educa-tion and reflects on some innovative practices. The contri-butors, from England, Northern Ireland, the Republic of Ireland and USA, all draw on research and practice in schools and in teacher education to reflect on key questions relating to educa-tion for citizenship in multicultural democracies.

Part 1 of Teachers, *Human Rights and Diversity* examines citizenship agendas and the context of teaching and learning for citizenship in England, the United States, Northern Ireland and the Republic of Ireland. In chapter 1, I discuss some of the tensions and challenges faced in educating for democratic citizenship in contexts of diversity, examining universal human rights, the recognition of difference, and structural inequalities. I draw on the Parekh report *The Future of Multiethnic Britain* (Runnymede Trust, 2000), the Crick report on *Education for Citizenship and the Teaching of Democracy in Schools* (QCA, 1998) and the report produced by the International Consensus Panel on Education for Global Citizenship in Contexts of Diver-sity (Banks *et al.*, 2005) to examine a vision of a future multi-cultural society and some principles which might inform education for citizenship in such a society.

In chapter 2, Carole Hahn provides us with a comparative analysis of the ways in which diversity and human rights are addressed in schools in England and the United States, drawing on data from the International Association for the Evaluation of Educational Achievement (IEA) study. She discusses the political contexts in which teaching and learning take place, before reporting on student attitudes in each country. The chapter concludes by identifying challenges for teachers and teacher educators, noting that students in England learn more about religious diversity than do their peers in the US, but are less likely to be aware of the contributions which minority communities have made to history than their US counterparts. Significantly, students in England do not 'routinely consider the challenges faced by ethnic/racial minorities in realising their citizenship rights in post-World War Two Britain'. US schools study women's suffrage but give less attention to gender equality in contemporary society. Generally speaking, they neglect to place citizens' struggles for civil and political rights within a broader international context or judge the success of campaigns for justice and equality against international norms.

Chapters 3 and 4 focus on Northern Ireland but are of relevance to multicultural democratic societies generally and to post-conflict and deeply segregated societies in particular. In chapter 3 Trevor Lindsay and Joe Lindsay discuss the system of segregated schooling in Northern Ireland, whereby 92 per cent of Catholic children attend Catholic schools and 94 per cent of Protestant children attend Protestant schools, leading to a situation where 'it is not uncommon in Northern Ireland for young people to reach the age of maturity with little or no experience of people from the other religious tradition'. The authors discuss the development of integrated schools and their impact on young peoples' attitudes and levels of openness. Chapter 4 provides further information on the Northern Ireland context, discussing sectarianism, racism and the role of human rights institutions and human rights education (HRE) in building peace. The writers, Jackie Reilly, Ulrike Niens and Roisin McLaughlin, report on a HRE pilot project in schools, funded by the Northern Ireland Human Rights Commission and the Department of Education in Northern Ireland (DENI). They focus on students' understandings of human rights and the extent to which they are able to apply these principles when focusing on contentious issues; students' identities and attitudes to Britishness and Irishness; and their responses to the active learning methodologies adopted in HRE classes. The authors also report on teachers' responses to the project and identify some of the challenges facing teachers introducing human rights education.

In chapter 5 Colm Ó Cuanacháin analyses conditions in the Republic of Ireland, arguing that there needs to be an appropriate and planned educational response to support people in embracing economic development 'in a framework informed by justice, peace, equality, non-discrimination and inclusion'. He reviews recent curriculum reform and discusses the role of citizenship education in contributing to this goal. The chapter concludes with a brief case study of how HRE was introduced into a small multi-denominational primary school. Ó Cuanacháin concludes that a human rights school can thrive within the current Irish policy framework but that if schools are to promote active and outward-looking citizenship in which young people act in solidarity with those in other parts of the world, there will need to be training, structural reforms at school level and committed leadership from educators and support from society as a whole.

The debates taking place at national, regional and international levels about the need for cosmopolitan citizenship education which both recognises diversity and promotes solidarity and social cohesion are also taking place in local communities and schools. Part 2 of *Teachers, Human Rights and Diversity* focuses directly on the experiences and understandings of students and teachers. Chapters 6 and 7 both draw on the experiences of young people and schools in London. In chapter 6 Hilary Claire reports on her research with children in inner city primary schools to explore how the teaching and learning of history might contribute to children's social and moral development. She presented children with real ethical and moral dilemmas, faced by a range of historical characters. In this chapter she analyses children's responses to a range of dilemmas: Nelson Mandela's decision to take up armed struggle against apartheid;

Miep Gies, the Dutch woman who hid Anne Frank and her family from the Nazis during the Second World War; and Allen Jay, a young Quaker boy involved in helping slaves escape via the Underground Railroad from the Southern States of America in the mid-nineteenth century. Claire reports on the developing personal stances of the children, noting that none started from an empty ethical position, but based their decision-making on existing knowledge and experience and a desire to 'do the right thing', whether this was informed by pacifism, compassion, or by a sense of justice. She notes their ability to weigh evidence, consider alternative perspectives, and think hypothetically. She builds up a careful and convincing argument for developing history teaching and learning in order to help children consider the kind of world we live in and the kind of world we want, central issues in education for citizenship.

Chapter 7 is an account by Anne Hudson of an initiative in a London secondary school to develop citizenship education through the formal curriculum and by developing the school structures and ethos so that young people would be empowered to make a difference in school and in the wider local community. Through the formal curriculum, students were encouraged to investigate local concerns and to consider broader international questions, such as fair trade and media representations of the Iraq war. Students were encouraged to find solutions to problems and they presented their concerns and solutions to local decision-makers. They also worked with staff to develop student decision-making in school. Subsequently, some students became actively involved in community development initiatives. Hudson demonstrates how, during the course of the project, democratic dialogue was extended among students. They were not engaged in mere academic exercises but were encouraged to express their opinions on matters of national and international significance in order to influence the democratic process.

Chapters 8 and 9 focus on the experiences and understandings of teachers. In chapter 8 Jill Rutter draws on her experiences as a teacher educator responsible for a specialised course for future teachers of citizenship, to explore how teachers might develop the curriculum to empower young people to critically examine popular and media discourses about refugees. She usefully draws parallels between historical and current day constructions of refuges, illustrating how since 11 September 2001 and increased concerns about security, the asylum seeker is portrayed as a potential terrorist. Rutter outlines British government asylum policies and indicates the impact of these policies on asylum seekers and on local communities, explaining how refugee students' experiences in schools mirror what happens in the wider community. She draws on her research to suggest strategies which teachers and schools might adopt to challenge racism more effectively. It would appear that children's views about asylum seekers and refugees tend to be fluid and that while many hold negative attitudes, others voice their support for these groups. She identifies the characteristics of schools that are able to challenge racism and promote diversity, indicating the importance of working with parents as well as children and suggesting activities which are likely to promote empathy and solidarity.

Rutter's work is complemented by that of Chris Wilkins, who in chapter 9 explores teachers' attitudes towards teaching in a multicultural society and their perceptions of their roles in educating young citizens. Wilkins' research tracks a group of students training to be teachers in the mid-1990s through to 2003. He focuses in this chapter on their attitudes to race equality issues, their understanding of the changing nature of racism and the role which education can play in challenging it. He reflects critically on the school citizenship curriculum and the teacher education curriculum, arguing that effective citizenship education must be underpinned by a framework of human rights and an understanding of structural inequality. He concludes that teachers need to see themselves as agents of social change if they are to be effective citizenship educators, enabling children also to see themselves as genuine social agents able to shape the future.

References

Banks, J.A., McGee Banks, C.A., Cortes, C.E., Hahn, C., Merryfield, M., Moodley, K.A., Murphy-Shigematsu, S., Osler, A., Park, C., Parker, W.C. (2005) *Democracy and Diversity: principles and concepts for educating citizens in a global age*. Seattle, WA: Center for Multicultural Education, University of Washington.

Held, D. (1995) Democracy and the new international order, in: D. Archibugi and D. Held (eds.) *Cosmopolitan Democracy*. Cambridge: Polity Press.

Held, D. (1996) *Models of Democracy*. 2nd edition. Cambridge: Polity Press.

Held, D. (2001) Violence and justice in a global age. http://www.opendemocracy.net/debates/article-2-49-144.jsp (accessed 7 July 2003).

International Institute for Educational Planning (IIEP) (2005) *International Perspectives on Migrants and Education Policy*. Paris: IIEP/UNESCO.

Osler, A. (2005) Education for democratic citizenship: new challenges in a globalised world, in: A. Osler and H. Starkey (Eds.) *Language Learning and Citizenship: international perspectives*. Stoke-on-Trent: Trentham.

Osler, A. and Starkey, H. (2005) *Changing Citizenship: democracy and inclusion in education*. Maidenhead: Open University Press.

Osler, A. and Vincent, K. (2002) *Citizenship and the Challenge of Global Education*. Stoke-on-Trent: Trentham.

Qualifications and Curriculum Authority (QCA) (1998) *Education for Citizenship and the Teaching of Democracy in Schools*. The Crick Report. London: QCA.

PART 1
CITIZENSHIP AGENDAS

1

Looking to the future: democracy, diversity and citizenship education

Audrey Osler

The processes of globalisation have led to the development of multicultural nation states, characterised by growing diversity. The success of multicultural democracies depends on the degree to which they are able to value and draw strength from their diversity yet, at the same time, promote an overarching set of shared values, ideals and goals to which all can adhere (Banks, 1997). A successful multicultural democracy needs to ensure a shared feeling of belonging so that all can engage in the community of the nation and practice their citizenship on the basis of equality (Osler and Starkey, 2005). The challenge is to nurture diversity *and* to foster cohesion and unity. This chapter explores some of the tensions that arise from the dual goals of nurturing diversity and fostering cohesion within citizenship education programmes. It also reflects on tensions arising from the concept of citizenship itself, which has contested and sometimes exclusionary meanings.

Justice and democracy

It is important that members of all communities are able to contribute to the society and that all can enjoy its benefits.

3

People from all communities need to be engaged in the processes of democracy. The engagement of diverse groups in the political life of the nation appears to be one of the greatest challenges facing many multicultural democracies. It is relatively easy to see how the skills of migrants boost the workforce and the economy, or how businesses are able to flourish in international markets if they employ a diverse workforce with a range of skills and knowledge of different cultures. Cultural diversity can strengthen and revitalise the arts and the whole of society can benefit and be influenced by new foods and forms of entertainment. But the sharing of power requires a different kind of openness and a widespread recognition that democracy itself will be stronger when all have the opportunity to participate. It is in the interests of all that the principle that all citizens are of equal worth is translated into practice. A common sense of belonging requires that all should have access to decision-making processes and be able to contribute to debates.

In order to draw strength from diversity and for a democracy to flourish, much more is needed than the basic democratic structures. What is required is the building of a human rights culture where diversity is seen as a strength. Such a culture must include opportunities for all communities to engage in public debate and deliberation so that decision-making is informed not just by the perspectives of elected representatives and powerful elites, but also by the perspectives and experiences of all sectors of society, including those who are disadvantaged. Such decisions are more likely to address current injustices.

One of the key challenges is to create a real sense of belonging in the face of structural inequalities such as poverty and racism. Equality of dignity, which underpins human rights, cannot be translated from a principle to a sustainable reality in societies where there are deep structural social and economic inequalities. Greater participation and engagement (a deeper democracy) is likely to create a more just society, as well as greater cohesion and unity.

Within any multicultural democracy, human rights principles provide an important framework for debating differences and resolving conflicts. Human rights belong to us all, regardless of our formal citizenship status within a country. Democratic principles and practices are not innate, but must be learned. Education has a key role to play in realising a democratic society that is just and equitable and in enabling individuals and groups to work together to overcome the past and present inequalities and injustices which prevent some members of society from enjoying their rights and from contributing fully.

Multiculturalism, human rights and a vision of a future society

In 1998, the Runnymede Trust, an independent think-tank committed to promoting racial justice in Britain, established the Commission on the Future of Multi-Ethnic Britain. The Commission produced a report, *The Future of Multi-Ethnic Britain* (Runnymede Trust, 2000), usually referred to as the Parekh report, after its chair, Bhikhu Parekh. The Parekh report identifies six beliefs or principles, which underpin the development of a multicultural society and which are useful in helping to conceptualise education for citizenship and democracy in the context of diversity.

Equal moral worth
The first principle is that all people have equal moral worth, irrespective of colour, gender, ethnicity, religion, age or sexual orientation, and have equal claims to the opportunities they need to realise their potential and contribute to the collective well-being. The principle of equal moral worth is a fundamental feature of a democratic society:

> Democracy is more than just a system for organising the election of governments. It is also a theory that all citizens are of equal worth and that all should be able to participate in the making of decisions that affect them. (Runnymede Trust, 2000: 234)

Democracy is a way of living together. Democratic values can inform interpersonal behaviour and institutional cultures as well as the structures of a nation-state.

The substance of the Parekh report, examining such areas as policing and the criminal justice system; education; arts, media and sport; religion; health and welfare; employment; immigration and asylum; and politics and representation illustrates how this principle is undermined in a society where there are deep social and economic inequalities. In order for people to enjoy the respect that must follow the principle of equal moral worth, the Parekh report is advocating systemic reforms to a range of institutions, including the education system.

Membership of communities

The second principle is that citizens are not only individuals but also members of (overlapping) communities, based on religion, ethnicity, culture and region: 'Britain is both a community of citizens and a community of communities, both a liberal and a multicultural society, and needs to reconcile their sometimes conflicting requirements' (Parekh, in preface, Runnymede Trust, 2000: ix). This principle raises the question of group rights as well as individual rights. Generally speaking, it is individuals, rather than groups, who are holders of rights. Some models of multiculturalism privilege difference yet ignore the fact that cultural groups cannot exist in isolation. It is important to consider the features of cultural groups or communities within a multicultural democracy:

■ memberships are not fixed (in a democratic State individuals must have the right to exit a community)

■ group values and practices change over time

■ diversity exists within cultural communities

■ inequalities exist within cultural communities

■ members of particular cultural communities are also members of other communities, including the multicultural community of the nation.

Under a model proposed by Kymlika (1999) cultural groups are given rights which he calls 'external protections' in order to reduce their vulnerability to the economic or political power of the larger society and to correct historical injustices. Such rights can include:

Language rights, guaranteed political representation, funding of ethnic media, land claims, compensation for historical injustice or the original devolution of power. All of these can help to promote justice between ethnocultural groups, by ensuring that members of the minority have the same effective capacity to promote their interests as the majority. (Kymlika, 1999: 31-32)

Kymlika goes on to argue that 'internal restrictions' on group members must be disallowed so as to protect potentially vulnerable members of the group in question, including women. Some feminists have expressed particular concern that liberal forms of multiculturalism ignore the diversity and particularly the inequalities that exist within cultural communities. Okin (1999), for example, has expressed concerns that the allowance of certain types of group rights are likely to undermine the position of women and to undo the gains made by feminists over recent decades. She is, in my opinion, rightly suspicious of extreme forms of multiculturalism which privilege group rights at the expense of basic universal human rights principles. She suggests that the model proposed by Kymlika is inadequate and that to allow group rights is not only to allow unacceptable practices against women but also to overlook the ways in which the structures of social institutions, including schools, present distorted representations of gender and gender relations serve to oppress women. These kinds of reservations are addressed to a large degree in the Parekh report which emphasises a shared commitment to democratic and human rights values as a minimum requirement for a multicultural democracy.

Charles Taylor, in a thoughtful essay on *The Politics of Recognition* (1994), discusses the need for recognition of cultural groups within multicultural societies in order to fully address the issue of equal dignity. He considers whether the institutions of liberal democratic government need to allow for the distinctive traditions of different cultural groups. He argues that protection needs to given to the basic rights of all citizens and that this often involves addressing inequalities by discriminating in favour of those who are disadvantaged. This position is similar to that adopted by the Parekh report, when it argues that to treat different people with different needs in the same way is necessarily unequal. Taylor points out that to support the collective goals to which some cultural groups aspire is not to advocate separatism or to be equated with trying to preserve particular cultures indefinitely. He concludes, like the Parekh report that:

> A society with strong collective goals can be liberal ... provided it is also capable of respecting diversity, especially when dealing with those who do not share its common goals; and providing it can also offer adequate safeguards for fundamental rights. There will undoubtedly be tensions and difficulties in pursuing these objectives together, but such a pursuit is not impossible, and the problems are not in principle greater than those encountered by any liberal society that has to combine, for example, liberty and equality, or prosperity and justice. (Taylor, 1994: 59-60)

Difference

Third, is the principle of difference. The Parekh report asserts that since individuals have different needs, equal treatment means that account must be taken of relevant differences. When equality insists on uniformity of treatment, it leads to injustice and inequality. This principle highlights a weakness of the Crick report on education for citizenship in England (QCA, 1998). The government-commissioned Crick report urges tolerance of minorities by the majority population, but it does not discuss the need for equality of rights. Tolerance is an important first step in establishing a multicultural democracy but needs to be supplemented by guarantees of equality of rights and the absence of discrimination, not just at the level of interpersonal relationships but also within the structures of government, the workplace and in service provision, such as housing, health and education. The Crick report focuses on national identity and on 'common citizenship' but ignores structural inequalities. Instead, it emphasises the need for cohesion and integration (Osler, 1999 and 2000a). Diversity is not generally recognised as a strength; indeed, the inference in the emphasis and frequency of references to 'difference' suggests that diversity is somewhat problematic and that it is more significant than our common humanity (Osler, 2000a). Nor does Crick discuss ethnicity in relation to inequality or differences in power

(Osler and Starkey, 2001). In other words, relevant differences are not taken into account.

Balance of diversity and unity

The fourth principle is that of recognising that diversity and unity are linked. As stated at the beginning of this chapter, a multicultural society must both nurture diversity and foster a common sense of belonging and a shared identity among its members. Although the Crick report quotes Modood and Berthoud's (1997) report for the Policy Studies Institute, which recommends that 'an explicit idea of multicultural citizenship needs to be formulated for Britain' (QCA, 1998: 3.15, 17), there is no discussion within the Crick report of the *relationship between unity and diversity* in a multicultural democracy. Instead, Crick stresses cohesion (unity). The Parekh report acknowledges the overarching democratic political community of the nation, and reaffirms the importance of human rights as clear normative values within a democratic community. It does not legitimate all practices on the grounds that they form part of a particular culture but recognises that all cultures are subject to change and to evaluation, against an agreed set of democratic and human rights norms. Just as, at a global level, all nations are subject to the same agreed human rights standards, so the community of the nation establishes a set of normative democratic standards, to which all individuals and constituent communities within the nation are subject. There is a common system of justice which applies to all.

There is complexity, and a degree of tension and possible ambiguity within the principle of recognising a balance between diversity and unity. The notion of difference, and respect for and celebration of difference, is only possible if all parties (individuals and communities) are subject to a minimal set of agreed common rules. Certain common or universal provisions underpin the recognition of difference and are guarantees that particular communities (and the members of those communities) are not disadvantaged merely because their cultural values differ from those of the majority. So, for example, no-one should be denied the right to hold public office or access to education merely because they adhere to a set of religious or cultural values which require them to observe specific dress or dietary codes. Such codes do not impinge on their ability to do the job or prevent them from participating in a learning community. In such cases, it is the workplace or school which may need to re-assess its rules or traditions, to ensure they are not exclusive of certain groups. Regardless of their cultural values, all will need to accept a minimal set of agreed common rules, which will include a commitment to democratic values. So, for example, an individual who failed to uphold democratic values and who denied the equality of dignity of all, might be denied public office.

These universal provisions also protect individuals and seek to prevent injustice within communities. Therefore, restrictions on the freedom of women or children cannot be justified on the grounds of traditional cultural values which deny them a voice or place them in a subordinate position. Balancing diversity and unity in this way addresses one of the problems inherent in an extremely liberal form of multiculturalism. The normative position, maintained in the Parekh report, differs from the relativist position of those multiculturalists who justify unacceptable practices, such as forced marriage or child marriage, on the grounds of respect for cultural difference.

Human rights and respect for deep moral differences
The fifth principle builds on the fourth, recognising human rights as providing a shared body of values but stressing that society must also respect deep moral differences and find ways of resolving inescapable conflicts. Parekh confirms that 'human rights principles provide a valuable framework for handling differences' but also emphasises the importance of 'essential procedural values such as tolerance, mutual respect, dialogue and peaceful resolution of differences' (Runnymede Trust, 2000: ix).

Figure 1.1 illustrates the basic concepts of human rights as identified by Starkey (1992), drawing on the European Convention on Human Rights and Fundamental Freedoms (1950) (ECHR), which is itself based on the Universal Declaration of Human Rights (UDHR) 1948. The ECHR is incorporated into UK

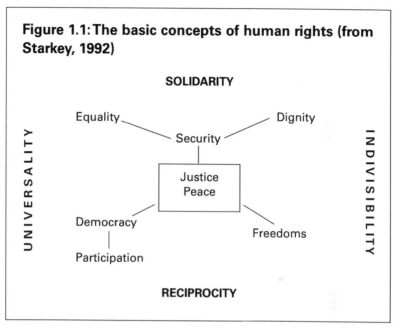

Figure 1.1: The basic concepts of human rights (from Starkey, 1992)

law through the Human Rights Act 1998. Starkey emphasises the importance of justice and peace (the goals of human rights as expressed in the preamble to the ECHR) by adopting them as the central focal point. In practice, the realisation of justice and peace in the world is through effective participative democracy. This form of democracy guarantees fundamental freedoms, such as freedom of expression and freedom of peaceful assembly and association. A denial of such freedoms is a denial of the ability to participate.

Democracy and freedoms alone are not enough to guarantee justice and peace, since unrestricted freedom could lead to exploitation and chaos; equality, rights and dignity are also set in place, in tension with freedoms. Finally, Starkey draws our attention to the concepts of reciprocity, universality, indivisibility and solidarity:

> They are reminders that the system is for all people (universality), that an attack on any part of the system is an attack on the whole system (indivisibility)... It is also a social system, and one which can only operate where there is a sense of mutual interdependence (reciprocity) and where people are prepared to take into

account and, indeed, defend the rights of others (solidarity). (Starkey, 1992: 127)

Procedural values such as tolerance, mutual respect, dialogue and peaceful resolution of differences are based on respect for the equality of dignity of each individual. Security is guaranteed when rights are protected and defended (including through the law) and when individuals engage in dialogue, showing the respect and tolerance which follow recognition of equality of dignity. Democracy and participation are central concepts within human rights which can only be maintained with due regard to such procedural values. Thus, human rights not only provide us with a framework for handling difference, as the Parekh report suggests, but also support the procedural values essential for peaceful resolution of differences within a multicultural democracy.

In schools, we can use this model to develop an approach which allows young people to see themselves as part of the total community (unity) while respecting their differences and taking account of relevant differences so as to ensure genuine equality. It is crucial however that young people are able to make interconnections between these concepts and experience (Carter and Osler, 2000). Human rights must engage teaching and learning 'in, for and about human rights' across the school, not simply in the isolation of the classroom (Heater, 1984; Lister, 1984; Starkey, 1984; Cunningham, 1991 and 2000).

The Council of Europe has provided guidance in applying human rights through education, effectively proposing a human rights school:

> where participation is encouraged, where views can be expressed openly and discussed, where there is freedom of expression for pupils and teachers, where there is fairness and justice. (Council of Europe, 1985, reprinted in Osler and Starkey, 1996: 183)

The Council of Europe framework emphasises both content and process, referring to knowledge, skills, values and social participation. Knowledge alone is likely to be inadequate; experience is crucial. Human rights education is a project which ideally needs to be espoused by all; it should not be restricted to students and teachers but should seek to include parents and other members of the community (Carolan, 2000).

Recognising racism

The sixth and final principle in the Parekh report recognises the 'subtle and complex phenomenon' of racism as 'an empirically false, logically incoherent and morally unacceptable doctrine'. The report stresses the need to address racism, stating:

> It may be based on colour and physical features or on culture, nationality and way of life; it may affirm equality of human worth but implicitly deny this by insisting on the absolute superiority of a particular culture; it may admit equality up to a point but impose a glass ceiling higher up. Whatever its subtle disguise and forms, it is deeply divisive, intolerant of differences, a source of much human suffering and inimical to the common sense of belonging lying at the basis of every stable political community. It can have no place in a decent society. (Runnymede Trust, 2000: ix)

Racism is not simply a moral issue. It serves as a barrier to participation and is thus an anti-democratic force. The doctrines and programmes of political parties espousing racist values serve to undermine democracy and human rights (Osler and Starkey, 2002 and 2005). Although the Crick report on education for citizenship and democracy ignored racism as an anti-democratic force, the British government has since identified citizenship education as a vehicle for promoting race equality (Home Office, 1999; Osler, 2000b) and, following the Race Relations (Amendment) Act 2000 (RRAA), requires schools and other public bodies to demonstrate to inspectors how they are promoting race equality (Osler, 2002; Osler and Morrison, 2002; Osler and Starkey, 2002). Intergovernmental organisations such as the European Commission and the Council of Europe make a strong case for antiracism as an essential element of democracy, with education seen as having a key role:

> Europe is a community of shared values, multicultural in its past, present and future;

> ...Full and effective implementation of all human rights without any discrimination or distinction, as enshrined in European and other international human rights instruments, must be secured;

Racism and racial discrimination are serious violations of human rights in the contemporary world and must be combated by all lawful means;

Racism, racial discrimination, xenophobia and related intolerance threaten democratic societies and their fundamental values;

Stability and peace in Europe and throughout the world can only be built on tolerance and respect for diversity;

...All initiatives aiming at greater political, social and cultural participation, especially of persons belonging to vulnerable groups, should be encouraged. (Council of Europe, 2000, my emphasis)

At the UN World Conference Against Racism held in Durban, South Africa in 2001, the European Commission stressed the need for both legislation and education to combat racism:

The fight against racism is now firmly rooted in European law. Specific reference to the fight against racism is contained in the Treaty establishing the European Community...

We know though, that there are many areas of discrimination that cannot be tackled by law. Practical action is needed to reach out to people and to help change the underlying prejudices that fuel racist attitudes and behaviour. Education is called to play a fundamental role in this endeavour. (Anna Diamantopoulou, European Commissioner)

Antiracism is thus essential to democracy. It is only by linking antiracism to democracy rather than exclusively to multiculturalism that it can be realised.

The six principles of the Parekh report are designed as the basis of dialogue and discussion about a vision of Britain as a multicultural democracy. They might also be the starting point for debate about citizenship within any multicultural democracy and about the features of a programme of education for democratic citizenship in multicultural contexts. The Parekh report did not rely solely on the perspectives of a few eminent citizens but also took evidence from a wide range of communities across the country. The Commission on Multi-Ethnic Britain provides us with a model of consultation and shows what can be achieved when citizens from a range of communities participate in providing evidence and in the deliberations and drafting of the recommendations. The Parekh report is able to look forward and to imagine a different future. It stands in contrast to the Crick report which does not appear to have consciously sought to include the perspectives and experiences of individuals from a wide range of cultural communities.

Multiculturalism and education for democratic citizenship

It is helpful to compare the principles from the Parekh report with those formulated by an international Diversity, Citizenship and Global Education Consensus Panel established by the Center for Multicultural Education at the University of Washington from 2003-2004. The panel was charged with the task of examining principles and concepts appropriate to citizenship education in a globalised world. It has produced a report *Democracy and Diversity: principles and concepts for educating citizens in a global age* (Banks *et al.*, 2005), which includes a useful checklist for schools. The panel identified four key principles and ten concepts or interrelated concepts for citizenship education. This report complements the Crick report in that it addresses questions relating to education for democratic citizenship, but focuses explicitly and centrally on questions of diversity, multiculturalism and global interdependence. It also complements the Parekh report, in that it provides pedagogical insights which fell outside the brief of the Commission on Multi-Ethnic Britain.

Unity and diversity

The first principle in the *Democracy and Diversity* report is that 'Students should learn about the complex relationships between unity and diversity in their local communities, the nation and the world'. The report suggests that students should examine how nation states address the limits of both unity and diversity as well as how the status of citizenship is defined and obtained in their own country and others. There is the assumption within the report that diversity and unity are indeed linked (Parekh, principle 4) and the recognition that the status and understanding of citizenship varies between nation states. Implicit in understanding the question of citizenship from a comparative perspective is that a critical understanding of one's own society and one's own culture requires one also to examine critically other cultures, contexts and arrangements (Figueroa, 2000).

Students are expected to consider how nation-states address inequality, and how members of different nation-states have dealt with the multiple identities of individuals, considering major social categories such as race, ethnicity, religion, gender and sexual orientation. The report states:

> Citizens in democratic multicultural nation-states endorse the overarching ideals of the nation-state such as human rights, justice, and equality and are committed to the maintenance and perpetuation of these ideals. Democratic citizens are also willing and able to take action to close the gap between these ideals and practices that violate them, such as social, racial, cultural, and economic inequality. Consequently, an important goal of citizenship education in a democratic multicultural society is to help students acquire the knowledge, attitudes, and skills needed to make reflective decisions and to take action in order to make their nation-state more democratic and just. (Banks *et al.*, 2005)

The *Democracy and Diversity* report also recognises that in tackling these issues there must also be a recognition that all are of equal moral worth (Parekh, principle 1); that, citizens are members of (overlapping) communities (Parekh, principle 2); that in dealing with inequalities, account needs to taken of difference (Parekh, principle 3); that, in a multicultural democracy, achieving a balance between unity and diversity not only requires a shared commitment to human rights but also respect for deep moral differences and an open, just and peaceful way of resolving conflicts (Parekh, principle 5). In addressing inequalities and multiple identities, the *Democracy and Diversity* report acknowledges racism as an anti-democratic force which needs to be addressed (Parekh, principle 6), listing it with 'prejudice' and 'discrimination' as among the ten concepts students should examine. The emphasis is on *action* to realise human rights, justice and equality.

Global interconnectedness

The second principle in *Diversity and Democracy* is that: 'Students should learn about the ways in which people in their community, nation and region are increasingly dependent upon other people around the world and are connected to the economic, political, cultural, environmental and technological changes taking place across the planet'. It is acknowledging the increasing interdependence which is taking place as a result of globalisation. This principle includes enabling students to examine the power of individuals and, particularly, groups to effect change through collaboration and co-operation. The goal is for students not only to grasp the complexity of the world but also to provide them with a sense of agency and to enable them to acquire skills and knowledge to help shape their communities, the nation and the world (Osler and Starkey, 2005).

Since diversity and interdependence exist at all levels from the local to the global, it is important that they are addressed at all these levels. Inequality and injustice also exist at these different levels. There has sometimes been a tendency for teachers to stress cooperation and interdependence at the level of the classroom and local community without acknowledging (and addressing) inequalities at this level. Similarly, when we move to the global level, there has been the tendency to emphasise others' problems or lack of human rights, without examining how global relationships are based on power differentials (Osler and Vincent, 2002). What is needed is education for cosmopolitan citizenship, which addresses diversity at local, national and international levels, while at the same time engaging with the concerns of young people themselves (Osler, 2005; Osler and Vincent, 2002; Osler and Starkey 2005). The need for education for cosmopolitan citizenship, which involves exploring these interconnected and complex issues, has in our post-September 11 world, become all the more urgent.

Human rights

The third principle in the Diversity and Democracy report is that: 'The teaching of human rights should underpin citizenship education courses and programmes in multicultural nation-states'. As the report states:

It is important when teaching for citizenship in contexts of diversity that the values which schools promote should have wide acceptance and legitimacy from an authority higher than any individual government or particular religion. Internationally agreed human rights standards provide a set of principles from which a school community can establish a set of shared values. These standards have an authority beyond any code of ethics at the national level and are consistent with the objectives of education for citizenship in societies, nations, and a world community characterised by diversity.

The community of the school is likely, as a public institution, to have as members, people with diverse cultures and beliefs. It is, like the nation, a community of communities. At the level of the institution, human rights provide a set of agreed principles from which shared values and rules can be agreed and conflicts and differences addressed.

In many multicultural democracies, teachers will have students in their classrooms who do not hold citizenship status (see Rutter, this volume). Citizenship is, however, a process and a practice as well as a status (Osler and Starkey, 2005). The status of citizenship is exclusive. An individual either holds citizenship status or not. The practice of citizenship cannot depend on status but on respect for others on the basis of our shared humanity and as equal holders of rights. As one submission to the Commission on the Future of Multi-Ethnic Britain put it:

> Human rights, being universal by definition, are not the privilege of citizens but the entitlement of all individuals ... It is not a shared passport which motivates individuals to respect human rights and the corresponding responsibilities but a shared humanity. (Runnymede Trust, 2000: 90)

Experience and participation

The fourth and final principle directly addresses a pedagogical approach which underpins education for democracy: 'Students should be taught knowledge about democracy and democratic institutions as well as be provided opportunities in which they can practice democracy'. The emphasis here is on knowledge and experience: 'If students are to learn democracy, they need to participate in it as well as learn it'. The report suggests that students should address: the history of democracy, the forces which have frequently caused its demise (such as tyranny of the majority, apathy, war), and the struggles of peoples for equal rights and inclusion.

The report also stresses that students should be participating in democracy at school: decision-making about school life, school governance and policy making. The report addresses the importance of deliberation or decision-making discussion, weighing up alternatives to decide the best course of action (Hahn, 1998; Parker, 2003). Furthermore, educators should pay special attention to content, pedagogy and climate. This will include looking at issues about which citizens disagree. The experience of democracy in schools is something which several of the chapters in this volume also explore.

Schooling, democracy and participation

Schools have the potential to contribute to the development of a multicultural democracy. Yet, as a number of chapters in this book illustrate, schools are part of the problem as well as part of the solution. Schools run on authoritarian lines do little to prepare their students for democratic participation and may do much harm (Harber, 2004) even if they have in place formal courses in education for democratic citizenship . Students are quick to identify contradictions when they are taught that democracy is a good thing yet it is not applied in the community of the school. As Hudson (this volume) has observed, the development of democratic school processes requires a school principal who is willing to take risks to implement changes which give young people more say in school decision-making. Segregated schooling systems, as have operated and continue to operate in Northern Ireland, have served to support a segregated society, where dialogue is difficult and where distrust and suspicion of the other is allowed to flourish (Lindsay and Lindsay, this volume).

Conclusions

Programmes of education for democratic citizenship in multi-cultural societies require teachers and students to face some of the contradictions and tensions of citizenship. While citizenship can be conceived as inclusive it is also used to exclude. The inclusive side of citizenship refers to universal human rights. All are included in this definition of a community of citizens. It is not only national boundaries but other factors, linked to gender, class and ethnicity which can serve to exclude. An internationalist and multi-layered perspective requires individuals not only to concern themselves with the quality of life within their own national boundaries, but also with human rights concerns elsewhere in the world. In devising education programmes, teachers will need to address the need to balance the tensions between recognising diversity; constructing or sustaining common political values and common bounds; and enabling young citizens to develop cosmopolitan perspectives in which they not only identify with the issues and concerns facing their own communities and the country in which they are living, but are also encouraged to recognise their common interests and common humanity with people living in other parts of the world.

References

Banks, J. A. (1997) *Educating Citizens in a Multicultural Society*. New York: Teachers College Press.

Banks, J. A., McGee Banks, C.A., Cortes, C.E., Hahn, C., Merryfield, M., Moodley, K.A., Murphy-Shigematsu, S., Osler, A., Park, C., Parker, W.C. (2005) *Democracy and Diversity: principles and concepts for educating citizens in a global age*. Seattle, WA: Center for Multicultural Education, University of Washington.

Carolan, S. (2000) Parents, human rights and racial justice, in: A. Osler (Ed.) *Citizenship and Democracy in Schools: diversity, identity, equality*. Stoke-on-Trent: Trentham.

Carter, C. and Osler, A. (2000) Human rights, identities and conflict management: a study of school culture through classroom relationships, *Cambridge Journal of Education*, 30 (3): 335-356.

Cunningham, J. (1991) The human rights secondary school, in: H. Starkey (Ed.) *The Challenge of Human Rights Education*. London: Cassell.

Cunningham, J. (2000) Democratic practice in a secondary school, in: A. Osler (Ed.) *Citizenship and Democracy in Schools: diversity, identity, equality*. Stoke-on-Trent: Trentham.

Figueroa, P. (2000) Citizenship education for a plural society, in: A. Osler (Ed.) *Citizenship and Democracy in Schools: diversity, identity, equality*. Stoke-on-Trent: Trentham.

Hahn, C. L. (1998) *Becoming Political: comparative perspectives on citizenship education*. Albany: State University of New York Press.

Harber, C. (2004) *Schooling as Violence: how schools harm pupils and societies.* London: RoutledgeFalmer.

Heater, D. (1984) *Human Rights Education in Schools: concepts, attitudes and skills* DECS/EGT (84) 26. Strasbourg: Council of Europe.

Hudson, A. (2005) Citizenship education and students' identities: a school-based action research project, in: A. Osler (Ed.) *Teachers, Human Rights and Diversity: educating citizens in multicultural societies.* Stoke-on-Trent: Trentham.

Home Office (1999) *Stephen Lawrence Inquiry: Home Secretary's Action Plan.* London: Home Office.

Kymlika, W. (1999) Liberal Complacencies, in, J. Cohen, M. Howard and M. C. Nussbaum (Eds.) *Is Multiculturalism Bad for Women?* Princeton, NJ.: Princeton University Press.

Lindsay, T. and Lindsay, J. (2005) Integrated education in Northern Ireland: the impact on children's attitudes, in: A. Osler (Ed.) *Teachers, Human Rights and Diversity: educating citizens in multicultural societies.* Stoke-on-Trent: Trentham.

Lister, I. (1984) *Teaching and Learning about Human Rights* DECS/EGT (84)27. Strasbourg: Council of Europe.

Modood, T. and Berthoud, R. (1997) *Ethnic Minorities in Britain: diversity and disadvantage.* London: Policy Studies Institute.

Okin, S. M. (1999) Is multiculturalism bad for women? in, J. Cohen, M. Howard and M. C. Nussbaum (Eds.) *Is Multiculturalism Bad for Women?* Princeton, NJ.: Princeton University Press.

Osler, A. (1999) Citizenship, democracy and political literacy, *Multicultural Teaching* 18 (1): 12-15 and 29.

Osler, A. (2000a) The Crick Report: difference, equality and racial justice, *Curriculum Journal*, 11 (1): 25-37.

Osler, A. (2000b) School inspection and racial justice: challenges facing OFSTED and schools, *Multicultural Teaching*, 19 (1): 22-27.

Osler, A. (2002) Citizenship education and the strengthening of democracy: is race on the agenda? in: D. Scott and H. Lawson (Eds.) *Citizenship, Education and the Curriculum.* Westport: Greenwood.

Osler, A. (2003) Crick Report and the future of multiethnic Britain, in: L. Gearon (Ed.) *Learning to Teach Citizenship in the Secondary School.* London: Routledge.

Osler, A. (2005) Education for democratic citizenship: new challenges in a globalised world, in A. Osler and H. Starkey (Eds.) *Language Learning and Citizenship: international perspectives.* Stoke-on-Trent: Trentham.

Osler, A. and Morrison, M. (2002) Can race equality be inspected? Challenges for policy and practice raised by the OFSTED school inspection framework, *British Educational Research Journal*, 28 (3): 327-338.

Osler, A. and Starkey, H. (1996) *Teach Education and Human Rights.* London: David Fulton.

Osler, A. and Starkey, H. (2001) Citizenship education and national identities in France and England: inclusive or exclusive? *Oxford Review of Education*, 27 (2): 287-305.

Osler, A. and Starkey, H. (2002) Education for citizenship: mainstreaming the fight against racism? *European Journal of Education* 37 (2): 143-159.

Osler, A. and Starkey, H. (2005) *Changing Citizenship: democracy and inclusion in education.* Maidenhead: Open University Press.

Osler, A. and Vincent, K. (2002) *Citizenship and the Challenge of Global Education.* Stoke-on-Trent: Trentham.

Parker, W. C. (2003) *Teaching Democracy: unity and diversity in public life*. New York: Teachers College Press.

Qualifications and Curriculum Authority (QCA) (1998) *Education for Citizenship and the Teaching of Democracy in Schools. Final report of the Advisory Group on Citizenship*. 22 September. (The Crick Report). London: QCA.

Runnymede Trust (2000) *The Future of Multi-Ethnic Britain. The Parekh Report*. London: Profile Books.

Starkey, H. (1984) *Human Rights Education in Schools in Western Europe*, Vienna, May 1883 (DECS/EGT (84) 25. Strasbourg: Council of Europe.

Starkey, H. (1992) Teaching for social responsibility, in: J. Lynch, C. Modgil and S. Modgil (Eds.) *Cultural Diversity and the Schools: human rights, education and global responsibility*, Vol. 4. London: Falmer.

Taylor, C. (1994) The Politics of recognition, in: A. Gutmann (ed.) *Multiculturalism: examining the politics of recognition*. Princeton, NJ: Princeton University Press.

2

Diversity and human rights learning in England and the United States

Carole Hahn

Many educators in multicultural democracies such as the United States and the United Kingdom advocate teaching about diversity and human rights. Committed teachers in these countries teach about the histories and cultures of diverse groups and about international human rights principles, documents and case studies. Such teachers realise that teaching about such topics is important, yet not sufficient. In addition to wanting their students to acquire knowledge, they want young people to develop skills, attitudes, and values that will enable them to become caring, participating citizens in societies that value diversity and respect human rights.

Importantly, educators recognise that young people need to learn about and for diversity and human rights in classrooms, schools, communities, and nations that are diverse and have the potential to foster human rights. This chapter draws upon Lister's (1984) model 'about, for and in human rights education' in which he argued that teaching *about* human rights, *for* the securing and maintenance of these rights, needs to take place *in* schools that are themselves characterised by a respect for

23

human rights. Here, I extend Lister's framework of teaching about, for, and in human rights to both diversity and human rights. In order to facilitate such teaching, teachers need a sense of what students bring to the classroom. In this chapter I discuss research from England and the United States that sheds some light on students' understandings of diversity and human rights and on their attitudes towards these principles. I draw primarily on the results of the Civic Education Study conducted by the International Association for the Evaluation of Educational Achievement (IEA) in which students from England and the United States, along with their peers in 26 other countries, were assessed on their civic knowledge, attitudes, and experiences (Baldi *et al.*, 2001; Kerr *et al.*, 2002; Schagen, 2001; Torney-Purta *et al.*, 2001).

Although diversity and human rights exist simultaneously and complement one another, like the two halves of a yin and yang symbol forming one whole, for the purposes of this chapter, I discuss them separately. First, I briefly introduce the IEA study. Secondly, I consider the elements of the research which address teaching and learning about, for, and in diversity. I then present those research findings related to teaching and learning about, for, and in human rights. Finally, I identify several areas that warrant attention by teachers and teacher educators.

The IEA Civic Education Study

The IEA Civic Education Study was carried out in two phases. In phase one, scholars gathered data from multiple sources to develop case studies of the contexts in which young people acquire civic knowledge, skills, and attitudes. The case study authors tried to ascertain what students were likely to be learning in three domains: democracy, national identity, and social cohesion and diversity. Data collected for the three domains provide useful insights into the contexts in which young people learn about diversity and human rights.

At the time of the study in 1999, citizenship education was not yet a statutory curriculum subject in England. Researchers in England reviewed the literature on citizenship education, analysed national curriculum documents for their citizenship content and interviewed experts in civic education (Kerr, 1999). The case study did not examine local education authority (LEA) documents on equality and diversity, nor did it address national initiatives in this field. In the United States, colleagues and I surveyed the 50 states, conducted content analyses of textbooks, and conducted focus groups with students aged 13 to 15 years and with teachers in four different states (Hahn, 1999a).

For phase two of the IEA Civic Education Study, researchers assessed nationally representative samples of students in 28 countries, enrolled in the modal year for 14-year-olds. Additionally, the students completed a questionnaire designed to measure their concepts, attitudes, and civic-related experiences. In all, nearly 90,000 students took part, including 3,043 students in 128 schools in England and 2,811 students from 124 schools in the United States (Baldi *et al.*, 2001; Kerr *et al.*, 2002). In this chapter, I discuss findings from the tests and questionnaires administered to Year 9 students in England and the United States in October 1999, as well as considering the qualitative data used in the case studies.

Teaching and learning about diversity

The case study of England reported on the prevailing political context which had influenced debates about citizenship education in the late 1980s and early 1990s, noting that discussion of national identity and social cohesion and diversity had often included arguments about the desirability of a national history or literary canon and the extent to which minority group perspectives and cultures should be incorporated into the school curriculum. The study noted how those advocating political literacy, antiracist education, and other initiatives to promote social justice had often met criticism from political opponents (Kerr, 1999).

Although there have also been debates in the United States about the extent to which schools should balance social cohesion and diversity, there has been a general consensus since the end of the nineteenth century that schools have a role in integrating immigrants and should educate young people for citizenship in a multicultural democracy (Hahn, 1999a). Citizenship education is recognised as a central purpose of schooling. The social studies curriculum, which draws largely on history and the social sciences, is viewed as a key vehicle for citizenship education. In addition, other curriculum subjects, school ethos, and out-of-school experiences also serve to teach young people about democracy, national identity, social cohesion and diver-sity. The picture is somewhat complex, however, because state boards of education and local school boards determine the curriculum and set standards for student achievement. Although voluntary national standards in social studies, history, and civics/government were developed in the 1990s, it is not clear how much influence these standards have had on what is actually taught in schools. Nevertheless, there is much similarity across the country due to tradition and the use of textbooks produced for a national market.

Many children recite a daily pledge of allegiance to the national flag in which they refer to 'liberty and justice for all'. Students are also taught that the founding document for their country, the Declaration of Independence, asserts that all people are created equal (Hahn, 1999a). Yet children's commitment to equality and justice runs deeper than one would expect from participation in a school ritual or hearing about a 200-year-old document. Their sense of justice is reinforced through history, where commonly in grades 5 and 8 (aged 10 and 13 years), they study a chronological narrative of the United States that tends to emphasise stories of struggles and progress toward democratic ideals. Concern for equality and justice is further reinforced through annual school celebrations of Martin Luther King Junior's birthday in January and Black History Month in February.

In focus groups, United States students said they learned about diversity in a variety of lessons: Native Americans and their forced removal in the nineteenth century; African Americans during slavery, segregation, and the Civil Rights movement; and women in the colonial period and the fight for women's suffrage in the nineteenth and early twentieth centuries (Hahn, 1999a). Textbook analysis confirms that authors focus on these topics. Additionally, textbook authors emphasise that the United States is a 'nation of immigrants' and focus on periods of the nation's history when there was considerable migration (Avery and Simmons, 2001).

Interestingly, it was only in Texas that students talked in focus groups about the history of Latinos and only in the Northwest that teachers mentioned teaching about the histories of Asian Americans (Hahn, 1999a). The textbooks and voluntary national curriculum standards in history and civics/government give almost no attention to Asians and Latinos (Avery and Simmons, 2001; Gonzales *et al.*, 2001) despite the fact that these groups have been part of the fabric of United States society for more than 150 years and are the fastest growing segments of the population. The IEA textbook analysis confirms studies by other researchers that, although women are mentioned more frequently in the textbooks of the 1990s than in earlier periods, they are still presented far less often than their male contemporaries. Indeed, the ratio of men to women was 16:1 in a range of widely used civics and history books for students aged 12 to 15 years (Avery and Simmons, 2001).

Religious diversity is an important aspect of cultural diversity. Traditionally, United States students learn about past struggles for religious freedom in social studies and history lessons. They also study landmark Supreme Court cases that dealt with the application of the First Amendment to the Constitution's guarantee of religious freedom. However, they tend to be taught little about the religious diversity in the United States today. In contrast, students in England have a range of opportunities to learn about the multi-faith nature of their society in school assemblies and religious education lessons (Hahn, 1999b). I have seen British children of all ages respectfully discussing different religious beliefs and practices and the views of atheists and agnostics. Such discussions are rare in United States schools, except perhaps in middle and high school courses in world geography when students might talk about beliefs associated with predominant religions in other countries.

Overall, United States students tend to learn about the historic contributions of diverse racial and ethnic groups and individuals, as well as about discrimination against various groups. Learning about diversity in contemporary society also occurs through their experiences in schools and communities characterised by diversity. In focus groups, students placed emphasis on learning through socialising with students from differing backgrounds in sports teams, the school band and through participation in other extracurricular activities (Hahn, 1999a).

Teaching and learning in contexts of diversity

The IEA Civic Education Study revealed that, both in England and the United States, young people from different socio-economic and racial/ethnic groups are not achieving equally in citizenship education. In England, students with fewer books at home and those with less educated fathers tended to have lower scores on the civic knowledge and skills parts of the test than other students (Schagen, 2001). In the United States, students with the fewest home literacy resources (books and newspapers) performed less well than students with many such resources (Baldi *et al.*, 2001). Similarly, students whose parents had little education performed less well on the knowledge test than students whose parents had more education. Students who attended schools with the highest percentages of students eligible for the free and reduced lunch programme did less well than students attending school with fewer students who were eligible for the programme (Baldi *et al.*, 2001).

Similarly, inequalities of achievement by race and ethnicity were apparent in both countries. Among British students, Black Caribbean students scored on average less than white students on the knowledge test and Indian students scored on average less than white students on the items measuring civic skills (Schagen, 2001). Students born in the UK and students speaking English at home tended to have higher scores on both the knowledge and skills scales than other students. In the United States, African American and Hispanic students had significantly lower knowledge scores than did white non-Hispanic and Asian students (Baldi *et al.*, 2001). In both England and the

United States, there were no overall gender differences in civic knowledge. However, on the skills scale, female students in both countries scored significantly above male students (Baldi *et al.*, 2001; Kerr *et al.*, 2002).

The study revealed some interesting differences in civic attitudes as well as knowledge for particular groups of students. On the attitude toward the nation scale in England (containing items such as 'the country should be proud of what it has achieved' and 'the country's flag is important to me'), Black Caribbean, Black African, Indian, Pakistani, and 'Other' students from minority backgrounds tended to have lower scores than white students (Schagen, 2001). In the United States, there were no differences between white and African American student responses to this scale (Baldi *et al.*, 2001). However, Hispanics and students born outside the United States were less positive toward the nation than non-Hispanics and students born in the United States.

The IEA Civic Education Study provides some information that educators may need to consider in teaching in multicultural classrooms in both countries. First, there are differences in achievement according to socio-economic status and ethnic group, in tests of civic knowledge and skills. Secondly, in both countries, white students reported more positive attitudes toward their country than did students from minority ethnic groups, with the exception that in the United States there were no significant differences between white and African American students.

Educating for diversity: student attitudes

It was not possible, within this comparative study, to ascertain students' attitudes towards specific racial, ethnic, and linguistic groups. However, the study does address attitudes towards the political and economic rights of immigrants and women, since these issues can be addressed cross-nationally. Students in most countries were supportive of immigrants' rights. Nevertheless, it was possible to detect some national differences in this generally positive picture. British students, overall, scored below the international mean, whereas students in the United States scored above the international mean (Torney-Purta *et al.*, 2001).

Moreover, some groups of students in both countries were significantly less favourable than others towards rights for immigrants. In both England and the United States, smaller percentages of male than female students supported rights for immigrants (Baldi *et al.*, 2001; Kerr *et al.*, 2002). In England, ethnic minority students tended to have higher scores than white students on the immigrants' rights scale (Kerr *et al.*, 2002). Among United States students, Hispanic, Asian and multiracial students had higher scores than white non-Hispanic students. Students who were themselves migrants had higher scores than those born in the United States (Baldi *et al.*, 2001).

Most students across countries participating in the IEA Civic Education Study tended to be supportive of women's political and economic rights. Students in both England and the United States scored significantly above the international mean on the women's rights scale, which contained items such as 'women should run for office and take part in government just as men do' and 'men and women should get equal pay when they are in the same jobs' (Torney-Purta *et al.*, 2001). In both countries, larger percentages of female than male students agreed or strongly agreed that women should have political and economic rights (Baldi *et al.*, 2001; Kerr *et al.*, 2002; Torney-Purta *et al.*, 2001). In England, students speaking English at home had higher scores on this scale than those who did not speak English, as did those with more books at home (Kerr *et al.*, 2002). Additionally, in England, students of Pakistani heritage were more supportive of women's rights than white students – a finding that may contradict some teachers' expectations (Schagen, 2001). In the United States, students born in the country were more supportive of rights for women than were students born outside and white students were more favourable than African-American students (Baldi *et al.*, 2001). Additionally, students with more home literacy resources were more supportive of women's rights than were students with few resources. It is apparent that diverse groups of students are developing different attitudes towards diversity and not all groups of students are achieving equally well when it comes to acquiring knowledge and skills needed for democratic citizenship.

Teaching and learning about human rights

Over the years, numerous authors have written about the need to teach young people about human rights (Branson and Torney-Purta, 1982; Lister, 1984; Hahn, 1985; Osler and Starkey, 1996; Tibbitts, 1996; Fernekes, 1999; Osler and Vincent, 2002). However, little empirical data are available on what the typical student learns about human rights in school. The IEA Civic Education Study provides limited additional information. On the knowledge part of the civic education assessment, just two out of 38 items dealt specifically with human rights. In response to a question about the purpose of the Universal Declaration of Human Rights (UDHR), 81 per cent of British students and 80 per cent of American students answered correctly. In response to a question about rights that are included in the UN Convention on the Rights of the Child, 77 per cent of students in England and 79 per cent of students in the United States answered correctly. The international average for each of the two items was 77 per cent. It is perhaps surprising that students in the two countries did as well as they did on these basic tests, given the little emphasis that is given to these topics in most schools.

Over the twenty years that I have been visiting schools in England, I have observed a few personal social and health education (PSHE) lessons based on the UDHR (Hahn, 1998). It is possible that, with the new emphasis on citizenship, more schools will include this topic in their curriculum. In the United States, students learn about the United States Constitution and Bill of Rights and the Civil Rights movement. However, it is rare that these topics are set in the context of international human rights instruments such as the UDHR (Branson and Torney-Purta, 1982; Hahn, 1998 and 1999a; National Expert Panel, 1998).

Learning for exercising and respecting human rights

Human rights include the civil and political rights to participate in government, directly by standing for office and indirectly by voting for government officials. In addition, civil and political rights include the rights to petition one's government and to freedom of expression. Social and economic rights include rights to education, health care, and an adequate standard of living. Student responses to several scales on the IEA instruments provide some insights into what young people think about a range of human rights issues.

Students were asked whether they thought it was important or very important for an adult who is a good citizen to undertake particular activities, such as voting in every election, discussing politics, or working for human rights. The IEA researchers examined responses in terms of two different types of citizenship activities – the more conventional political activities, such as voting, showing respect for government leaders, knowing about the country's history, discussing politics, and joining a political party – and those exercised by activists in social movements. The social movement-related citizenship scale included items about helping people in the community, taking part in activities to promote human rights, and taking part in activities to protect the environment. Interestingly, students from England scored below the international mean on the two citizenship scales. In contrast, students from the United States scored above the international mean on both scales (Torney-Purta *et al.*, 2001).

Looking at subgroup responses to the two citizenship scales, several similarities emerge in the two countries. On the conventional citizenship scale, in both England and the United States, there were no significant differences by gender or race/ ethnicity (Baldi *et al.*, 2001; Schagen, 2001). In response to activities listed on the social movement-related citizenship scale, in both England and the United States, higher percentages of females than males said it was important or very important for a good citizen to participate in social movement activities (Baldi *et al.*, 2001; Kerr *et al.*, 2002). In both countries, there were no significant differences in responses by either race/ethnicity or number of books in the home on the social movement-related citizenship scale (Baldi *et al.*, 2001; Schagen, 2001).

The 14-year-old students were asked how active they thought they might be as adults in exercising their civil and political rights. Somewhat surprisingly, 85 per cent of United States students expected that they would vote in national elections, compared to 80 per cent of students in England who thought they would vote in general elections. This is curious because, in reality, the voter participation rate in the United Kingdom is traditionally much higher than that in the United States. As to other civil and political rights that students anticipated exercising as adults, in England 57 per cent thought they would collect money for a social cause and 45 per cent anticipated collecting signatures for a petition. In comparison, in the United States 59 per cent of students thought they would collect money for a social cause and 50 per cent anticipated collecting signatures. 39 per cent of United States students and 28 per cent of students in England anticipated participating in a non-violent protest (Torney-Purta *et al.*, 2001).

The 14-year-olds reported that they had already taken part in some civic activities. In England, 25 per cent said they had taken part in an activity to help the community and 55 per cent said they had collected money for a charity or social cause. In the United States, 50 per cent of the students said they had taken part in an activity to help the community and 40 per cent had participated in collecting money for a charity (the international averages were 18 per cent for community service and 28 per cent for charity fund raising). Notably, only 5 per cent of students in England and 6 per cent in the United States said that they had participated in a human rights organisation (Torney-Purta *et al.*, 2001).

Turning now from exercising civil and political rights, to attitudes supportive of ensuring social and economic rights, there were two scales used in the IEA study that indirectly revealed relevant information. Students were asked whether or not they thought it was the government's responsibility to take action in several areas. On an economy-related government responsibilities scale, students were asked if they thought it was the government's responsibility to keep prices under control; provide industries with the support they need; guarantee a job for everyone who wants one; reduce differences in income and wealth among people; and provide an adequate standard of living for the unemployed. Students from England scored above the international mean on this scale, whereas students from the United States scored at the mean (Torney-Purta et al., 2001). This difference is probably not surprising, given that socialist governments and political parties have been a normal part of the political scene in the UK but not in the United States.

In England, females were more likely to say that it was the government's responsibility to intervene to protect economic rights, whereas in the United States there were no gender differences among student respondents (Baldi et al., 2001; Kerr et al., 2002). In England, Black Africans and Black Others had higher scores on this scale than whites (Schagen, 2001). In the United States, Asian and Black students were more likely than their white peers to assert the government should be responsible for economic-related issues (Baldi et al., 2001). In both countries, there were no significant differences on this scale for students from differing socio-economic backgrounds.

On the society-related government responsibilities scale, students were asked if it should be the government's responsibility to provide free basic education for all; provide basic health care; provide an adequate standard of living for old people; and other society-related activities. In both England and the United States, females were more likely than males to say that government should be responsible for these society-related issues (Baldi et al., 2001; Kerr et al., 2002). Also, in both countries, students with more books at home were more likely to say that government should be responsible for society-related issues (Baldi et al., 2001; Schagen, 2001). Furthermore, in the United States, Asians and whites were more likely than Blacks to say that government should be responsible for social issues (Baldi *et al.*, 2001). In England, there were no differences by racial/ethnic group on this scale (Schagen, 2001).

Overall, the IEA study provides several insights into young people's learning for exercising and respecting human rights. Students in the United States were more likely than students in England to say that they thought being a good citizen involved exercising political rights both in conventional ways and through community action and social movements. Students in both countries thought that as adults they themselves would exercise political and civil rights by voting and raising money for social causes. They were less likely to think they would organise petitions. A majority of 14-year-olds in England had already raised money for a charity and a majority of students in the United States had participated in activities to help the community. With respect to ensuring social and economic rights, students in England were more likely than students in the United States to say that it was the government's responsibility to guarantee a number of these rights, with females in both countries more likely than males to see both social and economic rights as government responsibilities.

Learning in schools that foster human rights
The IEA study provided some information on students' experiences of classrooms and schools that model human rights principles. Responses to two scales give an indication of the extent to which young people think their classes and schools encourage them to engage in democratic discourse and decision-making. Items on the classroom climate scale asked students the extent to which they thought they were encouraged to express their views; whether teachers presented more than one view; whether teachers respected student opinions; and if teachers encouraged them to discuss political or social issues about which people have different opinions. Students in England scored at the international mean on this scale and United States students scored significantly above the mean (Torney-Purta *et al.*, 2001). In both countries, female students were more likely than males to believe that the classroom climate was open for discussion of diverse views (Baldi *et*

al., 2001; Kerr *et al.*, 2002). In both countries, there were no significant differences on this scale by race/ethnicity (Baldi *et al.*, 2001; Schagen, 2001). However, in both countries, students reporting fewer than ten books in their homes perceived a less open classroom climate than did students with more books.

On the confidence in school participation scale, students were asked whether they thought that students getting together in groups to promote school improvement and solve problems could make a difference. Students in both England and the United States scored at the international mean on this scale (Torney-Purta *et al.*, 2001). Females in both countries had greater confidence in school participation than did males. In a secondary analysis of the IEA data for the United States, colleagues and I found that experience of a democratic classroom climate and confidence in school participation were two variables that predicted support for women's rights and immigrants' rights (Hahn *et al.*, 2003).

Challenges for teachers and teacher educators

Findings from the IEA Civic Education Study inform our understanding of young people's learning about, for, and in human rights. When combined with what the study reveals about students' experiences of diversity, it is clear that we need more research that explores these themes in depth cross-nationally. In particular, the findings present teachers and teacher educators with a number of challenges as they seek to implement practices to support education for citizenship in multicultural democracies.

First, although important strides have been made in developing an inclusive curriculum that teaches about the histories and cultures of diverse peoples, there is still much to be done. In England, students tend to learn more about differing religious communities than their peers in the United States. Although students in England study more social history than their United States counterparts, they are not necessarily aware of the contributions of diverse ethnic and racial groups to British history, nor do they routinely consider the challenges faced by ethnic/racial minorities in realising their citizenship rights in post World War Two Britain. In the United States, students seem to be more aware of religious diversity and immigration in their country's past than in contemporary society. They study a national narrative in which they see individuals working for the improvement of society and for greater realisation of civil and political rights. However, these struggles are not, for the most part, placed in a wider context of people all over the world, struggling for the achievement of human rights, nor are the achievements of United States governments or citizens assessed against international human rights standards and agreements.

Teacher educators can ensure that pre-service teachers have opportunities to critically examine curricular guidelines, standards, syllabi, and textbooks to determine for themselves the degree to which the current curriculum is inclusive. Teachers may then decide that they need to supplement the existing curriculum with lessons addressing omitted or under-represented topics.

In recent years, much has been written about the need to teach culturally diverse students using culturally responsive peda-gogy (Irvine, 2003). The IEA study reveals that in the areas of citizenship, diversity, and human rights there are particular needs related to teaching students in diverse schools, com-munities, and nations. There is a need to address the achieve-ment gap in terms of civic knowledge. In both countries, students from ethnic and racial minority groups and students from low-income families and communities tend to do less well on tests of civic knowledge than their peers. Rather than bemoan this situation, researchers and educators need to determine what teachers are doing successfully in schools in which such gaps do not appear. Once researchers have identi-fied purposeful samples of schools in which students of colour do as well as their white peers, they can observe classes and interview teachers and students in those schools to identify promising practices. These practices can then be replicated by teachers in other schools.

We also need to learn more about the development of attitudes related to diversity. In particular, more research is needed to determine how and why differences in attitudes toward immigrants and women develop. In the meantime, we can only speculate. It is possible that the differences in attitudes between students in the United States and England to immigrants' rights might be explained, at least in part, by the differing traditions in teaching about immigrants. In the United States, students repeatedly hear the country described as 'a nation of immigrants'. Young children are taught to value the ideals embodied in the symbol of the Statue of Liberty, and throughout their schooling American students hear about the contributions of various immigrant groups to the country's history. The fact that males in both countries were less supportive of immigrants' rights than females may reflect differing gender socialisation in which females develop sensitivity to the Other. The finding that white students in the two countries tend to be less supportive of immigrants' rights than those from other ethnic/racial groups and those born outside the country may indicate that white and native-born students fear that giving rights to others will diminish rights for themselves or that they think that other groups should be acculturated into the dominant culture.

Schools in the United States do teach about the women's suffrage movement, but they give less attention to gender equality in contemporary society. In England, students also have history lessons on the women's suffrage movement in their country. Additionally, many schools in England present assemblies and have religious education (RE) or PSHE lessons on the theme of equal opportunities, in which students investigate the topics of stereotyping and discrimination with respect to gender (Hahn, 1998). However, it appears that in both countries there is little exploration of gender and politics or gender and the economy (Hahn, 1996; 1998). Teachers could plan lessons in which students research the barriers that women face in becoming leaders in politics and business.

The fact that females tended to support women's rights more than males might indicate female enthusiasm for rights for their own gender. Alternatively, the gender differences may indicate that some males assume that rights are a zero-sum game in which granting rights to females might reduce their own opportunities. Whatever the explanations, teachers need to realise that, as they teach about historic and contemporary immigration and gender issues, individuals in their classes are likely to approach the topics through very different lenses. Teachers need to consciously create a classroom climate in which diverse views on the subject can be openly expressed, heard, and explored in some depth.

The fact that classroom climate and confidence in school participation predicts students' support for both immigrants' rights and women's rights, at least for 14-year-olds in the United States, is promising. This preliminary finding suggests that, when teachers encourage young people to engage in the open discussion of social and political issues in lessons and give them opportunities to influence school decision-making, students develop attitudes supportive of human rights. Ethnographic research is needed in schools that make a conscious effort to model a respect for human rights in the ways they engage students.

As policy makers and practitioners undertake new efforts to enhance young people's civic knowledge and engagement, it is essential that they pay attention to issues of diversity and human rights. It is clear from the IEA Civic Education Study that there are numerous challenges that need to be addressed by thoughtful educators and citizens in multicultural democracies such as the United States and the United Kingdom.

References

Avery, P. G. and Simmons, A. M. (2001) Civic life as conveyed in U.S. civics and history textbooks, *International Journal of Social Education*, 15: 105-130.

Baldi, S., Perie, M., Skidmore, D., Greenberg, E. and Hahn, C.L. (2001) *What Democracy means to Ninth-graders: U.S. results from the international IEA civic education study.* Washington, DC: U.S. Department of Education.

Branson, M. S. and Torney-Purta, J. (Eds.) (1982) *International Human Rights, Society, and the Schools.* Washington, DC: National Council for the Social Studies.

Fernekes, W. R. (1999) Human rights for children: the unfinished agenda, *Social Education*, 63: 234-240.

Gonzales, M. H., Riedel, E., Avery, P. G., and Sullivan, J.L. (2001) Rights and obligations in civic education: a content analysis of the national standards for civics and government, *Theory and Research in Social Education*, 29: 109-128.

Hahn, C. L. (1985) Human rights: an essential part of the social studies curriculum, *Social Education*, 49: 480-483.

Hahn, C. L. (1996) Gender and political learning, *Theory and Research in Social Education*, 24: 8-35.

Hahn, C. L. (1998) *Becoming Political: comparative perspectives on citizenship education*. Albany: SUNY Press.

Hahn, C. L. (1999a) Challenges to civic education in the United States, in: J. Torney-Purta, J. Schwille and and J. A. Amadeo (Eds.) *Civic Education Across Countries: twenty four national case studies from the IEA civic education project (583-607)*. Amsterdam: IEA. ERIC document reproduction services, ED 431 705.

Hahn, C. L. (1999b) *Educating a Changing Population: challenges for schools*. Halle Institute Occasional Paper. Atlanta, GA: Halle, Emory University.

Hahn, C. L., Cheong, Y. F., and Karunungan, M. (2003) Unity and Diversity: ninth-graders' attitudes in the United States. Paper presented at the American Educational Research Association, Chicago, April.

Irvine, J. J. (2003) *Educating for Diversity: seeing with a cultural eye*. New York: Teachers' College Press.

Kerr, D. (1999) Re-examining citizenship education in England, in: J. Torney-Purta, J. Schwille, and J. A. Amadeo (Eds.) *Civic Education Across Countries: twenty four national case studies from the IEA civic education project (203-228)*. Amsterdam: IAE.

Kerr, D., Lines, A., Blenkinsop, S. and Schagen, I. (2002) *England's Results from the IEA International Citizenship Study: what citizenship and education mean to 14-year-olds*. London: DFES.

Lister, I. (1984) *Teaching and Learning about Human Rights*. Strasbourg: Council of Europe, School Education Division.

National Expert Panel (1998) Human rights, in: C.L. Hahn, M. Hughes and T. Sen (Eds.) *Responses to the Eighteen Framing Questions, a-f, volume II, IEA Civic Education study phase I: The United States* (46-47). Atlanta: Emory University. ERIC Document Reproduction Service ED 444 886.

Osler, A. and Starkey, H. (1996) *Teacher Education and Human Rights*. London: David Fulton.

Osler, A. and Vincent, K. (2002) *Citizenship and the Challenge of Global Education*. Stoke: Trentham.

Schagen, I. (2001) Attitudes to citizenship in England: multilevel statistical analysis of the IEA civics data. Paper presented to the British Educational Research Association, Leeds, September.

Tibbitts, F. (1996) On human dignity: the need for human rights education, *Social Education*, 60: 428-431.

Torney-Purta, J., Lehmann, R., Oswald, H., and Schulz, W. (2001) *Citizenship and Education in Twenty Eight Countries: civic knowledge and engagement at age 14*. Amsterdam: International Association for the Evaluation of Educational Achievement.

3

Integrated education in Northern Ireland: the impact on children's attitudes

Trevor Lindsay and Joe Lindsay

Introduction

The education of Catholic and Protestant children together is often seen as one way of solving sectarian division in Northern Ireland. Although the first integrated school opened in 1981, the proportion of children attending integrated schools, although growing, is still only 5 per cent. This gives an indication of the deeply seated reservations of the majority of the population towards this approach. This article outlines the development and characteristics of integrated education and reports on an empirical study which set out to assess the degree of openness towards people from the other main religious tradition expressed by children who attended an integrated primary school, compared with that of children who had experienced a non-integrated primary education.

Segregated schooling

It is not uncommon in Northern Ireland for young people to reach the age of maturity with little or no experience of people from the other religious tradition (Toner, 1994; Fraser and Morgan, 1999). While this is clearly due in part to residential segregation, a major contributory factor is the largely segregated system of education that predates the establishment of the country. Before the partition of Ireland, most schools were owned and managed by the churches and so it was a thoroughly segregated system that was adopted when the new State was established in 1922. Protestant schools were transferred to the State and became 'controlled', while the Catholic schools became 'maintained' and were funded by a combination of contributions from the Catholic community and government grant. This division of children continues today. In fact, 92 per cent of Catholic children attend Catholic schools while 94 per cent of Protestant children attend Protestant schools (Department of Education, 2001, cited in Gallagher, 2003).

Educational segregation in Northern Ireland starts with nursery provision and continues through primary and post primary schools. Connolly with Maginn (1999) demonstrate how children as young as three develop an understanding of categorisation on the basis of religion and are able to attach positive and negative values to the symbols of their own and of the other tradition. The role of parents in encouraging negative attitudes is recognised by Connolly and Healy (2003) and has at times drawn massive media attention as, for example, in the coverage of the dispute at the Holy Cross primary school in Belfast.

Gallagher (1999) identifies the two main hypotheses used to explain the role of segregated education in the conflict. The 'cultural hypothesis' suggests that children attending different schools are exposed to a culture that emphasises difference through the formal and hidden curricula. A number of studies demonstrate how subjects such as religious education and history have been taught quite differently and the significant differences in sporting activities (Gallagher, 2003). Murray's research (published in the early 1980s and cited in Gallagher, 1999) revealed differences in relation to ritual, symbols and ethos. For example, Protestant schools were more likely to arrange visits to State institutions such as police stations and fire stations and had closer links with administrative bodies in the educational system. Pupils were exposed to different symbols, such as religious artefacts in Catholic Schools and the Union flag and photographs of the monarch in Protestant Schools. For Murray, of particular significance was not so much the fact that the schools made use of these symbols but, more importantly, the meaning that they had for members of the other culture, who saw them as deliberate displays of antagonism and provocation.

The 'social hypothesis' by contrast, suggests that, regardless of the curricula, formal or hidden, the practice of segregating children, by its very nature, emphasises and validates difference and fosters mutual suspicion.

Pressure for change

Segregated education, while the norm, has not been universal. For a number of years, a small number of secondary-aged pupils crossed sectarian lines to attend grammar schools, particularly in rural areas where it could happen that the only easily accessible school was on the 'other side'. The discussions of a small group of Catholic parents whose children were attending the predominately Protestant Methodist College, Belfast, grew into a wider discussion of the needs of 'minority' pupils and led eventually to the formation of ACT (All Children Together) in 1974. This pressure group argued for changes in the system that would allow the existing one-denominational schools to become shared (Morgan *et al.*, 1992). It was hoped that existing schools could be persuaded to become integrated. Enabling legislation in the form of the Dunleath Act 1978 attempted to bring this about. This Act allowed schools to balance the religious composition of their Boards of Governors in the hope that the governing bodies would then institute other changes to bring about integration. When three years later no one had taken advantage of the legislation, disappointed parents took the initiative and set up the first integrated school at Lagan College in Belfast (Fraser and Morgan, 1999).

Development of integrated schools

Throughout the 1980s, integrated education grew slowly. This was due primarily to the fact that the legislation required the new schools to 'prove their viability', a process which involved the funding of capital and running costs from private sources, charitable trusts and foundations, a burden that exceeded £2.5million in the years between 1982 and 1990. The situation was eased with the passage of the Educational Reform (N.I.) Order 1989 (ERO). In many respects the ERO mirrored the Education Reform Act 1988, which applied only to England and Wales, but it also included special provision for Northern Ireland. A community relations dimension was included in the curriculum in the form of Education for Mutual Understanding (EMU) and Cultural Heritage Programmes. It also, for the first time, placed a duty on the Department of Education to encourage and facilitate the development of integrated education. This resulted in rapid expansion for the integrated sector, with the 50th integrated school opening in 2003.

A recent survey established there is widespread support for the concept of integrated education with 82 per cent of respondents saying that they personally support integrated education and 81 per cent saying that they see it as important for peace and reconciliation in Northern Ireland (NICIE, 2003). Nevertheless, only 5 per cent of the children of Northern Ireland are able to attend an integrated school.

Research in the 1990s indicated that the most common reasons for parents choosing a secondary school were the potential for academic achievement and career prospects. Only 7 per cent of parents of girls and 8 per cent of parents of boys gave 'mixed by religion' as the most important reason; 'many parents who choose not to send their children to integrated schools do so on educational grounds' (Miller *et al.*, 1996). However, in a more recent Omnibus survey 52 per cent of respondents said that the main reason for not sending their children to an integrated school was because there were none in the area. Less than half a per cent gave lower academic standards as the reason.

A complicating factor in parental choice is that, unlike the rest of the UK, Northern Ireland has retained selection on the basis of ability at the age of 11 years. While it seems clear from the Report of the Post Primary Review Body (Burns Report, 2001) that there is widespread support for the abolition of selection for secondary school on the grounds of ability, many parents are unwilling to take the risk of not sending their children to grammar school, as long as these schools exist. Many families experience great disappointment when their child fails to do well enough in transfer tests to obtain a place. However, since integrated schools are by far the main providers of mixed ability schooling in Northern Ireland, they take on the status of comprehensive schools. As such, they are perceived in some quarters as falling into the middle of the pre-existing hierarchy of schools, inferior to grammar schools but better than secondary schools. As the majority of children (about 70 per cent) do not obtain a grammar school place, many parents are likely to view mixed ability integrated schools as an attractive educational option.

Features of integrated schools

Murray (1993) outlines the distinctive educational ethos of integrated schools which differ from other schools in a number of ways. First, they are set up by parents who own them in a way that parents in other schools do not. There is an expectation among parents that the approach taken by the teachers will be less traditional. Parents expect a broader education and they expect to be more closely involved, with stronger links between home and school. Secondly, since the schools have been set up with the express purpose of educating children together, there is an emphasis on children valuing and respecting people who are different from themselves. This valuing of diversity extends well beyond encouraging respect for people of the other religion. Integrated schools are integrated not only by religion but are also co-educational and integrated by ability and social class. They bring together pupils from all sections of the community, Catholic and Protestant, rich and poor, rural and urban. This provides them with a rich resource, a cross-section of society upon which teachers can constantly draw, in and out of the classroom. Teachers are very aware of the fact that they have children from different traditions in class and this in turn helps them to think in a more pluralistic way.

Integrated schools adopt an anti-bias curriculum (ABC) which has developed out of a collaborative parent/teacher project and focuses on the processes and judgements by which attitudes develop (Hovey, 1993). It is based on the understanding that children as young as two years have acquired the prejudices and stereotypes on which they base their attitudes and behaviour (Connolly, 1998). Consequently integrated schools have chosen to target the nursery classes to begin a whole-school ABC development. The curriculum is considered in its widest sense and focus is placed on each and every aspect of the educational experience, both formal and informal.

Integrated education draws on three related models of learning: 'contact', 'deficiency' and 'balance' (Rowley, 1993). The contact model is based on the assumption that bringing children together will in itself lead to changes in how they perceive each other. The deficiency model assumes that children form negative opinions of each other through misconceptions, based on ignorance and lack of information. The balance model is a development of the contact model and proposes that every school should be balanced in terms of staffing, parents, pupils and governors. Drawing on the work of Carl Rogers, Rowley (1993) suggests a fourth model, the contextual. He argues that an individual's ability to understand and accept an alternative view is dependent upon how the person values him/herself. Only by accepting oneself can one learn to accept others. The concept of self-esteem is at the core. An individual's sense of self is related directly to the process of primary socialisation, the preconditions of which are the Rogerian principles of empathetic understanding, unconditional positive regard and genuineness. These are also the preconditions for the therapeutic environment necessary for a child's personal growth and, according to Rowley, must underpin the ethos of the school and all concerned with it, parents, teachers and governors. According to this model, an integrated school is necessarily child-centred; children must first accept themselves before they can accept others.

Opposition to integrated schools

The development of integrated education has not been without its opponents. Some members of the Catholic Church have argued that the religious ethos essential for the education of Catholic children cannot be provided in an integrated school. Consequently, some bishops and priests have either refused to admit pupils from integrated schools to the sacraments or imposed special conditions upon them. The Free Presbyterian Church has objected to Protestant children attending integrated schools on the grounds that they were being exposed to heretical doctrine. Others have argued that integrated schools draw funds in an unfair way from non-integrated schools or that they draw attention from the efforts of these schools to improve community relations through EMU and Cultural Heritage Programmes.

Researching children's attitudes

In spite of considerable research into impact of the troubles on the young, there has been little attention given to the effects of integrated education on young people's attitudes. We set out to investigate whether attendance at an integrated primary school had any impact on the attitudes of pupils towards people of the other religion. Our research draws on the framework of an earlier study into attitudes of young people in Northern Ireland (Greer, 1985).

Greer investigated the attitudes of children and young people (12 to 16 years) to members of the other religious tradition. He argued that, in terms of determining the attitudes of the young people, the concepts of prejudice and non-prejudice were problematic and that a measure of *openness* was more useful. An important aspect of prejudice is that it is determined by judgements being made about a group or an individual 'without sufficient warrant' (Allport, 1954). This is problematic since it is difficult to determine the extent to which a judgement is warranted. For people in Northern Ireland, this presents a particular dilemma since most people are both the victims and perpetrators of prejudicial attitudes and may hold negative attitudes as a consequence of experiences of violence, intimidation or discrimination. The concept of openness is defined as 'the willingness of pupils to value members of the other tradition as neighbours, relatives, workers and people worth knowing' (Greer, 1985: 279). Greer developed an openness scale that can be used in Northern Ireland to investigate the importance of gender, age and religious affiliation on young people's attitudes. He devised a six-item questionnaire that required responses on a Likert type scale across five points ranging from 'strongly agree' to 'strongly disagree'. The results were analysed in two ways. First, responses to each statement were expressed as percentages, making it possible to study the pattern of response. Secondly, the mean score was calculated for each pupil. This makes it possible to draw comparisons between different groups on the basis of age, gender and religious affiliation.

For the purposes of our study, we asked form teachers at an integrated secondary school to administer the questionnaire to all Year 7 pupils (aged 11-12 years). The teachers were provided with a statement about the survey, which they read out before the questionnaire was completed. This statement described the purposes to which the information would be put, gave assurances in respect of confidentiality and some guidance on how the form was to be completed. Ninety-eight out of the total 120 pupils were present on the day and completed the questionnaire. Three pupils completed the form incorrectly and their responses had to be disregarded. This left a total sample of 95, of which 44 had attended an integrated primary school and 51 had not.

Findings

Table 3.1 presents the children's responses to each item, represented as percentages. The questionnaire comprised four positive and two negative items. Responses to the positive items were scored 5 to 1 and to the negative items 1 to 5. As Table 3.1 indicates, there was a high degree of openness in both those

Table 3.1: Pupils' responses to the attitude statements in the openness scale expressed as percentages

Items	Strongly Agree %		Agree %		Not certain		Disagree %		Strongly Disagree %		No Answer %	
	IPS	NIPS	IPS	NIPS	IPS	NIPS	IPS	NIPS	IPS	NIPS	IPS	NIPS
I would be very unhappy if my brother or sister were to marry a person from the other religion	9.1	9.8	4.5	17.6	38.6	33.3	22.7	23.5	22.7	13.7	2.3	2.0
I would be quite happy if a family of the other religion moved in next door to me tomorrow	20.5	23.5	63.6	54.9	13.6	15.7	2.3	3.9	0.0	0.0	0.0	2.0
I would be quite happy to have someone of the other religion as my teacher	31.8	27.4	52.3	47.0	15.9	19.6	0.0	3.9	0.0	0.0	0.0	2.0
I think that in Northern Ireland, members of the two religions should be kept apart	9.1	3.9	6.8	5.9	13.6	25.5	18.2	43.1	50.0	21.6	2.3	0.0
I would like to learn more about the beliefs and worship of the people from the other religion	22.7	17.6	40.9	43.1	18.2	23.5	11.4	9.8	4.5	3.9	2.3	2.0
Pupils in Protestant and Catholic schools in Northern should have more chances to meet and mix	47.7	35.3	38.6	45.1	6.8	7.8	2.3	7.8	2.3	2.0	2.3	2.0

IPS (Pupils from Integrated Primary Schools) n= 44   NIPS (Pupils from Non-Integrated Primary Schools) n= 51 who attended an integrated primary school and those who had not. For example, 86 per cent of pupils who had been to an integrated primary and 80 per cent of those who had not felt that pupils in Catholic and Protestant Schools should have more opportunities to meet and mix. Eighty-four per cent of pupils who had been to integrated primary schools and 78 per cent of the others agreed that they would be quite happy if someone from the other religion moved in next door. Faced with the prospect of a brother or sister marrying a person of the other religion the percentage of pupils from non-integrated primary schools expressing unhappiness was nearly double that of pupils attending integrated schools, 27 per cent as against 14 per cent. Forty-five per cent of integrated primary school pupils, as against 37 per cent of non-integrated disagreed with the statement that such a marriage would cause them to be unhappy.

The second analysis was achieved by calculating mean scores for the whole scale, ranging from 30 to 6 for each pupil. The mean was then found for each group, allowing a comparison to be made of openness for the two groups (See Figure 3.1). This resulted in an openness rating of 23.23 for the pupils who had come from an integrated primary school, compared with a rating of 21.31 for those who had come from non-integrated

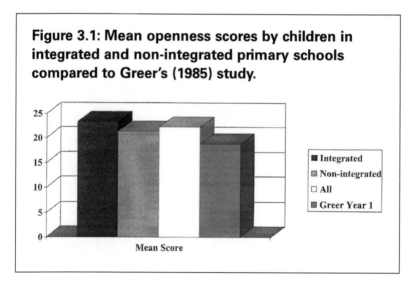

Figure 3.1: Mean openness scores by children in integrated and non-integrated primary schools compared to Greer's (1985) study.

schools and an overall mean rating of 22.20 for the whole group. The difference of 1.88 can be expressed as an 8.1 percentage increase. While this is not a huge difference, it is significant. As the ratings were arrived at using an identical calculation to that used by Greer, a comparison can be made with his findings. Greer calculated an overall rating for his sample of 20.27. However, account needs to be taken of the fact that he was using a wider range of respondents in terms of age and that he found that openness increased with age. His rating for Year 1 (equivalent of this sample) was 18.8.

The ratings for both pupils who had and those who had not attended integrated primary schools were higher than in Greer's study. There are two possible explanations. One is that attitudes in Northern Ireland generally have become more open over the two decades since his study. Another is that it could be expected that the parents who send their children to the integrated school have more open attitudes than the general population and pass these on to their children through the processes of socialisation.

Conclusion
Integrated schools in Northern Ireland have been set up by groups of parents, who have been unhappy about the prospect of their children being educated in ghettoised schools, seeing this as having a detrimental effect not only on their offspring but on Northern Irish society generally (Murray Cavanagh, 1993). A number of factors operate in how parents select schools. For some, probably a minority, having children educated together is of prime importance. For others, factors such as convenience of location, the school's reputation, and the preference of peers may take precedence. However, regardless of the diverse reasons that parents have for choice of school, the *raison d'etre* of integrated schools is their mixed nature and the impact that attending an integrated school has upon children in terms of how they view members of the other community. This study is limited by its focus on just one secondary school for which there is only one feeder integrated primary school. While it would not be safe to generalise from the

results, it does provide some indication that attendance at an integrated school may have some impact on how open pupils are to members of the 'other side'.

References

Allport, G.W. (1954) *The Nature of Prejudice*. Cambridge, Massachusetts: Addison-Wesley.

Burns Report (2001) *Education for the 21st Century: Report of the Review Body on Post-Primary Education*. Bangor: Department of Education.

Connolly, P. (1998) *Racism, Gender Identities and Young Children*. London: Routledge.

Connolly, P. and Healy, J. (2003) The development of children's attitudes towards 'the troubles' in Northern Ireland, in: O. Hargie and D. Dickson (Eds.) *Researching the Troubles: social science perspectives on the Northern Ireland conflict*. Edinburgh: Mainstream Publishing.

Connolly, P. with Maginn, P. (1999) *Sectarianism, Children and Community Relations in Northern Ireland*. Coleraine: Centre for the Study of Conflict, University of Ulster.

Fraser, G. and Morgan, V. (1999) *In the Frame: integrated education in Northern Ireland: the implications of expansion*. Coleraine: Centre for the Study of Conflict, University of Ulster.

Gallagher, T. (1999) *Schools for Justice, Schools for Hate: the role of education in social conflict*. Belfast: The Psychological Society, Northern Ireland Branch.

Gallagher, T. (2003) Education and equality in Northern Ireland, in: O. Hargie and D. Dickson (Eds.) *Researching the Troubles: social science perspectives on the Northern Ireland conflict*. Edinburgh: Mainstream Publishing.

Greer, J.E. (1985) Viewing 'the other side' in Northern Ireland: openness and attitudes to religion among catholic and protestant adolescents, *Journal for the Scientific Study of Religion*, 24 (3): 275-292.

Hovey, A. (1993) As easy as ABC: the anti-bias curriculum, in: C. Moffat (Ed.) *Education Together for a Change: integrated education and community relations in Northern Ireland*. Belfast: Fortnight Educational Trust.

Miller, R. Wilfird, R. and Donoghue, F. (1996) Attitudinal support for and low participation in integrated education; a Northern Ireland conundrum, *Administration*, 44 (3): 61-69.

Morgan, V. Dunn, S. Cairns, E., and Fraser, G. (1992), *Breaking the Mould: the roles of parents and teachers in the integrated schools in Northern Ireland*. Coleraine: Centre for the Study of Conflict, University of Ulster.

Murray, A. (1993) The educational ethos of an integrated primary school, in: C. Moffat (Ed.) *Education Together for a Change: integrated education and community relations in Northern Ireland*. Belfast: Fortnight Educational Trust.

Murray Cavanagh, C. (1993) Integrated schools and their impact on the local community, in: C. Moffat (Ed.) *Education Together for a Change: integrated education and community relations in Northern Ireland*. Belfast: Fortnight Educational Trust.

Northern Ireland Council for Integrated Education (NICIE) (2003) *Public Opinion Survey; integrated education in Northern Ireland*: Belfast: NICEI.

Rowley, T. (1993) contextual education: the Hazelwood College Model, in: C. Moffat (Ed.) *Education Together for a Change: integrated education and community relations in Northern Ireland*. Belfast: Fortnight Educational Trust.

Toner, I.J. (1994) Children of the 'troubles' in Northern Ireland: perspectives and intervention, *International Journal of Behavioural Development*, 17: 629-47.

4

Education for a Bill of Rights for Northern Ireland

Jackie Reilly, Ulrike Niens and
Roisin McLaughlin

The role of human rights education in the promotion of peace is recognised internationally, as confirmed by the UN Commission on Human Rights (2004) resolution on human rights education which establishes a World Programme and an international cooperation and government-civil society framework of cooperation:

> Convinced that human rights education is a long-term and lifelong process by which all people at all levels of development and in all strata of society learn respect for the dignity of others and the means and methods of ensuring that respect in all societies, and that human rights education significantly contributes to promoting equality and sustainable development, preventing conflict and human rights violations and enhancing participation and demo-cratic processes, with a view to developing societies in which all human rights of all are valued and respected. (UN Commission on Human Rights Resolution 2004/71)

In societies experiencing the legacy of ethno-political conflict and which are engaged in peace building processes, human rights education, institutions and legislation are often seen as tools for fostering a culture of peace and promoting positive inter-group relations; a perception which has been evident, for example, in reconstruction programmes in the Balkans and in South Africa (Rodley, 2001).

Conflict and segregation

Northern Ireland has a protracted history of ethno-political conflict between Nationalists/Republicans (of whom the majority are Catholics), striving for the unification of Northern Ireland with the Republic of Ireland and Unionists/Loyalists (of whom the majority are Protestants), striving to remain part of the United Kingdom. From the late 1960s, Northern Ireland experienced a renewed period of active inter-group conflict, referred to locally as 'the troubles'. The conflict has taken its toll on individuals and society, with over 3,523 deaths and many more people injured in the period between 14 July 1969 and 31 December 2001 (Sutton, 2003).

From 1993, Northern Ireland embarked on a peace process, eventually resulting in most paramilitary organisations declaring cessations of violence. In 1998, all of the main political parties signed the Belfast/Good Friday Agreement. In a referendum, held in Northern Ireland and the Republic of Ireland, 71 per cent of voters supported the peace process, with a voter turn-out of 81 per cent. The establishment of a devolved government (which is suspended at the time of writing) was one of the most visible and widely welcomed outcomes of the agreement. The Northern Ireland Act 1998 (Section 68) also established the Northern Ireland Human Rights Commission (NIHRC), set up the following year. The NIHRC's main task is to prepare a Bill of Rights for Northern Ireland and to advise the British government on what should be included in such legislation. Additionally, the NIHRC is committed to promoting a culture of human rights through education and research.

Despite these developments, Northern Ireland remains a deeply segregated society, with Protestants comprising 53 per cent of the population and Catholics comprising 44 per cent. Research suggests that sectarian attitudes have declined over the years (Hughes and Carmichael, 1998), yet results for the 2003 elections pointed to a polarisation of political attitudes, with the more politically extreme parties representing both unionist and nationalist communities making large electoral gains over their more moderate counterparts. Although Northern Ireland is sometimes described as an increasingly multicultural society, the proportion of people in the 2001 census who selected self-descriptors other than White was just 1 per cent; this compares with 9 per cent visible minorities in Britain (BBC, 2003a and 2003b). It may be explained, in part, by the impact of the conflict on immigration and the economy.

Concerns about racism in Northern Ireland have increased since the beginning of the peace process and there have been numerous and widely publicised reports of racially motivated attacks on members of ethnic minority communities. Indeed, 226 racial incidents were reported in 2002/2003. This represents an increase of 900 per cent since 1997 when racial incidents began to be recorded (CRC, 2003).

In response to concerns about racism, in 2002, the Office of the First and Deputy First Minister in the Northern Ireland Assembly commissioned a review of race and racism to assess the experiences and needs of ethnic minority people, in the context of current legislative and policy initiatives in the region. These initiatives include the Race Relations (NI) Order 1997;[1] the Northern Ireland Act 1998 (Section 73), which established the Equality Commission; and the Government's strategy of promoting social inclusion as part of its Targeting Social Need (TSN) agenda. The legal definition of racism, formulated in the Race Relations (NI) Order 1997, precludes sectarianism as a sub-category of racism because religion is not included in the definition of racial groups (Connolly, 2002a).

A debate has emerged in Northern Ireland as to whether sectarianism should be defined as a form of racism (Brewer 1992; McVeigh, 1995, 1998). Sectarianism has been located in a broader context of what have been called 'systems of subordination' (Smyth and Moore, 1995) which include sexism, racism and social class, insofar as all are based on notions of one group's superiority over another and rely on the ultimate threat of using violence to maintain the *status quo*. However, there is a surprising lack of research 'on the effect of sectarian-ism and the conflict in Northern Ireland on racism' (Connolly and Keenan, 2002: 344).

Education for peace and human rights

This chapter examines a pilot project to introduce human rights education, the Bill of Rights in Schools (BORIS) project. The first stage of the BORIS global and local human rights education pilot project took place in 24 secondary schools across Northern Ireland in 2003 and was funded by the NIHRC and the Department of Education for Northern Ireland (DENI). The project aimed to promote awareness of human rights issues in general and the proposed Bill of Rights for Northern Ireland in particular. The programme focused on five key human rights concepts: equality, freedom, justice, respect and participation. It was intended to address issues relating to diversity, including racial, religious and social diversity, en-compassing a range of groups, including, for example, people with disabilities and the homeless.

In each school, participating classes had between four and ten lessons, which were either taught by one of the five BORIS project research officers or by one of their teachers, with the support of a project officer. In this chapter we report on an external evaluation of BORIS, focusing specifically on the im-pact of the project on students' knowledge, attitudes and be-haviour and on teachers' perceptions of the project's impact, its relevance and its relationship to citizenship education.[2]

The BORIS project needs to be understood both in the context of the changing socio-political climate in Northern Ireland and in the context of broader developments in education policy which have come about as a result of the changing socio-poli-tical climate. While previous educational programmes, such as Education for Mutual Understanding (EMU), focused on im-proving relationships between Catholics and Protestants, new curriculum initiatives take a broader view of Northern Irish society (Gallagher and Smith, 2002). Multicultural/antiracist curricular initiatives have been identified as a key area for development. The new citizenship education programme being developed by the Council for the Curriculum Examinations and Assessment (CCEA) is highlighted as a potential tool for integrating multicultural and antiracist perspectives into the broader curricular framework (Connolly, 2002b).

Evaluation

The project evaluation team asked participating students to complete pre-project and post-project questionnaires, in order to make a quantitative assessment of the impact of the BORIS initiative. In total, 293 matched pre- and post-tests were returned from 16 of the 24 schools, including six controlled schools (mainly Protestant), eight maintained schools (mainly Catholic) and two integrated schools (mixed religion).[3] The total sample for pre- and post-test included 107 boys and 183 girls, while three students did not specify their gender. Ages ranged between 11 and 18 years (mean = 13 years). Questionnaires were distributed during class time, at the beginning and end of the BORIS project.[4]

The questionnaire was designed to highlight learning experiences and changes relating to knowledge and information-seeking behaviour; attitudes relating to the law, nationality and racism; and confidence in participation. Religious denomination was not measured as an individual variable, but was indirectly taken into account through classification of schools into maintained (Catholic), controlled (Protestant) and integrated (Catholic and Protestant). While this differentiation did not allow for a denominational distinction of students in integrated schools, it nevertheless provides a classification based on identity in the school context, consistent with suggestions that integrated schooling affects students' social identities (see Lindsay and Lindsay, this volume).

Additionally, interviews were carried out with individual participating teachers and with students in focus groups, all of which were conducted after the project had been completed. Four focus groups were conducted with young people, aged 13 and 14 years (total number = 45). One took place in an integrated school and a second in a school for children with special educational needs, both involving a mix of students by religion and gender. The remaining student focus groups were conducted in two maintained (Catholic) girls' schools. All discussions were taped and transcribed.

Semi-structured interviews were also conducted with the project co-ordinator, the five project officers and four teachers from participating schools (total number = ten). All were experienced teachers and had previous experience of related initiatives, for example, EMU and citizenship education.[5] The interview schedule focused on issues such as perceived strengths and weaknesses of the project (for example, in relation to training, outreach, overlap with other projects such as EMU and School Community Relations Programme), support mechanisms, implementation issues and the relationship between BORIS and citizenship education. Suggestions for future refinements and development of the project were also elicited.

Students' knowledge of human rights

The majority of students enjoyed participating in the BORIS project, with 72 per cent indicating that they enjoyed it 'a great deal' or 'quite a lot'. Similarly, 77 per cent of students stated that they had learned 'a great deal' or 'quite a lot' about human rights during the project. Pre- and post-test results were compared using statistical difference tests.[6] Table 4.1 presents the pre- and post-project results related to students' knowledge of human rights.

No significant changes were revealed regarding students' reading patterns relating to human rights, though watching TV items relating to human rights actually decreased during the time of the intervention. While this decrease in information-seeking behaviour may seem surprising, it has to be pointed out that the Iraq war broke out just before the intervention and this impacted on students' behaviour at pre-test stage. At the end of the BORIS project, when the post-tests were distributed, the war in Iraq had ended and TV news viewing patterns, which had been up about 5 per cent during the build-up to the war, had stabilised. The significant reduction in time spent watching human rights-related TV news at post-test stage probably reflects a generalised trend in the population. While discussions

Table 4.1: Information seeking behaviour, discussions and knowledge about human rights

Variable	Item	Sample and significance level	Pre-test Yes %	Pre-test No %	Post-test Yes %	Post-test No %
Information seeking behaviour	In the last two weeks, have you watched anything on TV (news item, documentary etc) relating to human rights?	N = 247**	83	17	75	26
	In the last two weeks, have you read anything (in a newspaper, magazine, website) relating to human rights?	N = 233	57	43	49	52
Discussions about human rights	In the last two weeks, have you talked to friends about human rights issues?	N = 237**	50	50	65	35
	In the last two weeks, have you talked to family members about human rights issues?	N = 239	47	53	47	53
Knowledge about human rights	Please write down any issue or concern relating to human rights that you are aware of.	N = 293**	41	59	70	30
	Please write down why you think Northern Ireland may get a Bill of Rights.	N = 293**	11	89	65	35
	Please write down the name of the organisation which talks to people in Northern Ireland about a Bill of Rights.38	N = 293**	0	100	38	62

Sample sizes differ due to missing data. Significance: ** = $p < 0.01$

Table 4.2: Pre-test and Post-test: Interest in human rights, socio-political attitudes and confidence in participation

Variable	Item(s)	Sample and significance levels	Pre-test Mean	Post-test Mean
Interest in human rights	How interested are you in human rights?	N = 246**	2.51	2.74
Attitudes to foreigners	People from other countries make Northern Ireland a better place.	N = 224**	2.13	2.56
	People from other countries who come here as refugees should not get the same advantages as people from Northern Ireland.	N = 232*	2.87	3.04
Attitudes to the law	The law should always protect the innocent even if it means sometimes guilty people go free because the evidence isn't good enough.	N = 222**	2.44	2.92
Attitudes to Irishness (scale, (a = .71)	The new law for Northern Ireland should make sure that people who feel Irish feel at home in Northern Ireland.	Controlled (N = 76) Maintained (N = 145) Integrated (N = 52)*	2.33 3.43 2.85	2.32 3.54 3.19
	Irish flags and the Irish language should not be promoted in Northern Ireland.			
Attitudes to Britishness (scale, (a = .67)	The new law for Northern Ireland should make sure that people who feel British feel at home in Northern Ireland.	Controlled (N = 76)** Maintained (N = 143)** Integrated (N = 51)	3.48 2.37 2.99	2.65 3.16 3.28
	British flags should not be promoted in Northern Ireland.			

Table 4.2: Pre-test and Post-test: Interest in human rights, socio-political attitudes and confidence in participation (continued)

Variable	Item(s)	Sample and significance levels	Pre-test Mean	Post-test Mean
Confidence in participation (scale, (a = .75)	How confident are you expressing an opinion when everyone else seems to disagree with you?	N = 270**	2.98	3.10
	How confident are you participating in discussions about human rights?			
	How confident are you participating in discussions about political issues?			
	How confident are you speaking out when you believe somebody has been treated unfairly?			
	How confident are you doing something to promote the human rights of other people?			

Response formats range from one to four. A higher number indicates more positive attitudes.

Sample sizes differ due to missing data.

Significance: * = p < 0.05 ** = 0.01

with parents about human rights issues remained stable, discussions with friends actually increased, which may be explained by Bill of Rights classroom activities.

In comparison to the pre-test, post-test results revealed significantly higher levels of knowledge about human rights issues in general and about the Bill of Rights for Northern Ireland in particular. For example, five respondents mentioned racism (or Black/White relations) in the pre-test yet in the post-test it was mentioned 26 times, suggesting an increased awareness. Similarly, sectarianism (or Catholic/Protestant relations) was mentioned three times in the pre-test in contrast to fourteen references in the post-test.

Students' attitudes and confidence in participation

Table 4.2 illustrates how students' interest in human rights and confidence in participation significantly increased during the intervention period. Attitudes towards foreigners also appear to have improved. This is, at first sight, somewhat surprising since short-term interventions do not generally have a major impact on attitudes (Allport, 1954; Trew, 1986). These results therefore need to be interpreted cautiously: young people in Northern Ireland may not necessarily experience normative pressures to display positive attitudes to ethnic minorities because of the relative lack of racial diversity in Northern Ireland. Consequently, participation in the BORIS project may simply have increased awareness of such social pressure rather than led to a significant change in attitudes.

Attitudes towards Britishness and Irishness were analysed separately for students from different types of schools. Interestingly, among students from controlled (Protestant) schools, attitudes towards Irishness remained stable, while attitudes towards Britishness significantly worsened. For students from maintained (Catholic) schools, attitudes towards Irishness remained stable, while attitudes towards Britishness significantly improved. For students from integrated schools, attitudes towards Irishness significantly improved, while attitudes towards Britishness did not improve significantly. The complex pattern relating to the impact of the project on sectarian attitudes is unsurprising. Sectarian attitudes are entrenched and sectarianism is seen as an inescapable feature of Northern Ireland society. Sectarianism is, however, more openly subject to social pressures (Cairns and Hewstone, 2002). A project such as BORIS, which sets out to challenge sectarian attitudes, may provoke a degree of uncertainty, as reflected in these results, rather than lead directly to more positive attitudes. The differences between schools need further exploration and need to be considered when reviewing teaching contents and materials.

Generally knowledge, attitudes and behaviour relating to human rights appear to have improved during the intervention period. Attitudes towards the law also became significantly more positive. As control group data were not available, improvements cannot be definitely attributed to the intervention programme. Nevertheless, the data from student and teacher interviews, discussed below, support the questionnaire analysis that the BORIS project had a positive impact on participants.

Students' experiences of human rights education

The 45 students who participated in focus group interviews unanimously agreed that they had enjoyed the project sessions, whether these had been conducted by a member of the project team alone or in conjunction with their own teacher. Specific mention was made of activities that particular classes had engaged in, such as a graffiti wall and a Bill of Rights for the classroom and specific classroom discussion topics, such as community relations and peace, other religions and cultures were also highlighted. While students praised individual project staff and their personal teaching styles, enjoyment of the sessions appeared to revolve around the content and active teaching and learning methods.

Most focus group participants agreed that they had known little about human rights at the outset of the project, as illustrated by this extract from one focus group:

Student 1: We didn't know very much about nothing really.

Student 2: Did anybody know anything?

Student 3:   No. They gave us this questionnaire, we didn't have a clue!

Interviewer: You didn't have a clue?

Student 2:   No, but we did it again [at the end of the project] and it was easy!

Another group who had previously received some human rights education in school also felt they had learned a lot in the course of the project. Students in one focus group emphasised learning about other countries, cultures, religions and people. They also stressed new knowledge related to specific rights (children's rights, freedom of expression) and to the responsibilities that are related to rights, as one student summed up:

> Different types of rights, for teachers as well as for us...rights for everybody really.

Students were asked if the project had changed their views in any way. Discussions around this varied in content but all agreed that they had been introduced to a new way of looking at both local and global issues. Some students mentioned that learning about human rights made them respect other people and encouraged them to: 'treat people like you want to be treated back'.

In one focus group, students were able to explain how they had applied human rights principles in considering relationships between Northern Ireland and other countries. Nevertheless, there appeared to be difficulties in transferring these principles and positive approaches to human rights when reflecting on the conflict in Northern Ireland. This was illustrated in discussions about controversial issues such as the display of national flags. National flags in Northern Ireland (British and Irish) are symbols of national identity which divide communities and demark territories. They can be threatening to anybody not associated with the national flag:

Student 1:   We done about.. He [teacher] told us about the differences, the same things about Northern Ireland and South Africa.

Student 2:   Different places.

Student 3:   And he tried using...

Student 1: Questions after, like he said questions and stuff. And all these worksheets and people have a right, if we fly our flag, then Protestants or Catholics should have a right to fly their flag.

Interviewer: And what did you think?

Student 1: No.

Interviewer: No? (group laughter)

Student 1: Yeah, they should like 'cause (...) if we have a right to, I think we should have a right to put them [flags] up, well not put them up but have a say and things, have a point of view. It might not be (something I agree with) but (they still have it).

There were also several examples of students independently applying a human rights framework to current affairs, for example, in a discussion within one group about a widely publicised incident during the Iraq war. Two of the focus groups raised specific local human rights issues and there was some rather light-hearted discussion of skateboarders' rights, which nevertheless illustrated that students were applying what they had learned to novel situations and problems. Focus group participants were also asked if they had behaved differently as a result of the project. Responses were varied, with one participant explaining that personal difficulties around a disabled sibling had been put in a new perspective.

Two groups had extremely lively discussions around the issue of Orange Order parades, which often commemorate British victories in historic battles against the Irish. These parades are often strongly opposed by Nationalist communities and have resulted in violence and community clashes. Drumcree represents one of the most controversial marches, which has been associated with widespread community disturbances over a number of years. In one focus group most students began by advocating a tolerant approach, even to contentious marches in interface areas. However, when one student voiced a less tolerant perspective, citing personal experience, others agreed and some strongly held opinions were voiced. Once again, some children appeared to have difficulties applying those human rights principles with which they were in general agreement to the situation in Northern Ireland. Their long-standing attitudes to local issues of conflict took precedence in determining behaviour:

Interviewer: ... did any of you get involved in the protests against the war against Iraq?

Student 1: No, just Drumcree.

Interviewer: Drumcree? So I mean you think that's a way of expressing yourself too?

Student 1: Aye. We were allowed to roadblock the roads 'cause the Orangemen [weren't allowed to march] at Drumcree and so [nobody] was allowed to [travel].

Student 2: Everybody should be allowed to, you know the way there's Orange marchers and the Black marchers and stuff like that, well there's one of them went right past our estate and no one said anything to them...

Interviewer: Well, would you be willing to say, for example, 'Okay, in order for everybody to get along, maybe the Orange marches shouldn't go ahead'?

Student 1: No. They should be.

Interviewer: Well, what do you think about the St. Patrick's Day parade in Belfast?

Student 1: No way.

Student 2: Aye.

Student 3: I don't like that there... [but] it's Protestant as well.

There were many indications that students perceived the BORIS project as having relevance to their own lives, as indicated by some of the examples cited above. All participants believed that all children should know about their rights and some had even advised other family members or friends as a result of the project. In addition, there was a general appreciation that knowledge of human rights was important in adult life, although it was often suggested that it was more important in careers which involved dealing with people such as nursing, social work or policing. Generally, students valued the participative teaching methodologies. They felt they had learned a lot and they appreciated the relevance of human rights to their own lives both now and in the future.

Teachers' perspectives

The teachers were generally in favour of the project and con-sidered it relevant to students, although in some cases they had been sceptical at the outset:

> And I have to say initially I thought 'Oh my goodness this is going to be well above these children. This is totally unrelated to their lives!' But the way it was taught and the way it was put across, it was very much more a citizenship approach and it was ground level and definitely [the project officer's] approach was suited to the need of the particular pupils.

Policy issues and teachers' needs

Teachers commented on the project's timeliness, with a new curriculum and citizenship education currently being intro-duced. There was consensus that human rights education, in-cluding education about the proposed Bill of Rights, was a natural element of citizenship education. Teachers also recog-nised that this was particularly appropriate to Northern Ireland given the post-conflict situation, although there was also clear support for similar human rights education initiatives in other contexts.

The project officers all agreed on the need for a planned, staged approach to teaching about the proposed Bill of Rights for Northern Ireland. They all suggested that it was necessary to introduce some global human rights education before pro-gressing to teaching about the local context. Both teachers and project officers reflected on teachers' needs in relation to the BORIS project and to human rights education more generally. Some project officers ran training sessions for teachers, where they introduced active teaching methods, such as circle time. The training confirmed that not all teachers knew enough about these methods or about human rights issues to teach effectively. One project officer voiced the dismay he felt when some teachers at a training session expressed the view that corporal punishment should be allowed in schools:

...in this day and age and they weren't only saying this to themselves but to their [the pupils'] parents, you know? I suppose I'm
bringing my own views to it, but I was quite shocked that some
people, educated people could think those sort of [things].

Throughout the project, there was variation in practice; some
teachers were supported by project officers in the classroom,
whereas other teachers observed project officers teaching their
classes. One important outcome of the project is the dissemina-
tion of innovative and interactive teaching methods, exercises
and activities in a range of schools. The need for active teaching
methodologies was given considerable emphasis by BORIS
project officers. The teachers felt that the subject matter was
inherently interesting for students and that the various
methods and activities fully engaged them:

And let me tell you it wasn't just the personality, because I mean
[the project officer] was special to them, they loved [the project
officer] but they did like talking about it. And it opened up, I mean
it amazed me – well I knew that [pupil] was quite sort of interested
but like, it showed you who listened to the news and who was
aware of what was going on in the world. *Teacher*

There was general support for a human rights culture in schools
and a recognition that this required a whole school approach.
Several participants, both teachers and project officers, mentioned school councils as a key tool for realising such a culture.
Interviewees were generally positive about the impact of the
project in enabling a human rights culture:

[The BORIS project is] a beginning, you know, I think we could
begin to get this culture into our schools. I think we certainly need
it here in Northern Ireland.

However, some interviewees also voiced what may be termed
'realistic ambivalence' on this issue. They noted that, in most
schools, students have relatively few responsibilities and suggested there may be limits to the feasibility of truly democratic
schools. Interestingly, some teachers observed that many
students were already aware of their rights and asserted them
readily, but were not so good at granting the same rights to
others.

Students' knowledge and attitudes

Teachers commented on how the project had provided students with time to reflect on human rights issues and the language or vocabulary for discussing them. The speed with which students had learned this language and had gained confidence in using it in discussions was also noted. One teacher, working with students with special educational needs, mentioned that, while students understood the teaching and could discuss key concepts in the classroom, there appeared to be a gap between knowledge and practice. She suggested that, outside the classroom, it was unlikely that one short-term project would have much impact on behaviour.

Teachers perceived the BORIS project to be a timely intervention both in terms of the political context of post-conflict Northern Ireland and in the education policy context, with the introduction of citizenship education. Additionally, teachers were unanimous in their assessment that students had enjoyed participation and had learnt a good deal. The project gave teachers the opportunity to share interactive teaching methodologies and materials. While there was support for a human rights culture in schools there was also recognition that the development of this culture was by no means unproblematic.

Conclusion

The quantitative and qualitative data collected for the evaluation of BORIS demonstrates that students enjoyed the project and that their knowledge about human rights issues and the Bill of Rights for Northern Ireland increased dramatically. Despite its short-term nature, the project has raised participants' awareness in relation to both racism and sectarianism as human rights issues.

There has often been a tendency within educational initiatives promoting peace in Northern Ireland to avoid addressing sectarianism and racism simultaneously. Terms such as 'tolerance' or 'mutual understanding' may well be inclusive of all ethnic and religious groups in society, but in practice have often translated to anti-sectarian approaches. This may reflect a perceived need in the immediate post-conflict period to address the causes of that conflict before tackling other social problems judged to be less urgent. There may be underlying assumptions that reducing one form of prejudice will 'naturally' lead to the reduction of other forms of prejudice. As social identity theory suggests, a change of outgroup is one possible strategy for groups under threat to maintain their self-esteem and the integrity of the group (Tajfel and Turner, 1979). In societies emerging from ethno-political conflict, it is therefore vital to address all forms of prejudice. Otherwise, the danger remains that new targets for prejudice may suffer the consequences. In Northern Ireland, the introduction of citizenship education represents one means by which this danger can be avoided. It is vital for future peace that tensions and prejudices are addressed, not only as they relate to the two major denominational communities but among all ethnic and religious communities (Arlow, 2001).

References

Allport, G.W. (1954) *The Nature of Prejudice*. Reading, Massachusetts: Addison-Wesley.

Arlow, M. (2001) The Challenges of Social Inclusion in Northern Ireland: citizenship and life skills. Paper presented at the Conference for Curriculum Development for Social Inclusion, Lithuania, December.

Brewer, J. (1992) Sectarianism and racism and their parallels and differences, *Ethnic and Racial Studies*, 15 (3) 352-64.

British Broadcasting Corporation (BBC) (2003a) *Ethnic Groups Growing – census*. http://news.bbc.co.uk/1/hi/uk/2756041.stm (accessed on 19.04.04).

British Broadcasting Corporation (BBC) (2003b) *Fascination of Religion Head Count*. http://news.bbc.co.uk/1/he/northern_ireland/2590023.stm (accessed on 19.04.04).

Cairns, E., and Hewstone, M. (2002) Northern Ireland: the impact of peacemaking on intergroup behaviour, in: G. Salomon and B. Nevo (Eds.) *Peace Education: the concept, principles, and practices around the world*. Mahwah, NJ: Larry Erlbaum Associates.

Community Relations Council (CRC) (2003) Press Release: http://www.community relations.org.uk/about_the_council/press_releases/31/ (accessed 30.01.04).

Connolly, P. (2002a) 'Race' and Racism in Northern Ireland: a review of the research evidence. http://www.research.ofmdfmni.gov.uk/raceandracism/section2.htm (accessed 30.01.04).

Connolly, P. (2002b) Researching young children's perspectives on 'the troubles' in Northern Ireland, *Child Care in Practice*, 8 (1) 58-64.

Connolly, P., and Keenan, M. (2002) Racist harassment in the white hinterlands: the experiences of minority ethnic children and parents in schools in Northern Ireland, *British Journal of Sociology of Education*, 23 (3) 341-356.

Gallagher, A.M. and Smith, A. (2002) Attitudes to academic selection, integrated education and diversity with the curriculum, in: M. Gray, K. Lloyd, P. Devine, G.

Robinson and D. Heenan (Eds.) *Social Attitudes in Northern Ireland: the eighth report.* London: Pluto Press.

Hughes, J. and Carmichael, P. (1998) Community relations in Northern Ireland: attitudes to contact and integration, in: G. Robinson, D. Heenan, M. Gray and K. Thompson (Eds.) *Social Attitudes in Northern Ireland: the seventh report.* Aldershot: Ashgate.

Lindsay, T. and Lindsay, J. (2005) Integrated education in Northern Ireland: the impact on children's attitudes, in: A. Osler (Ed.) *Teachers, Human Rights and Diversity: educating citizens in multicultural societies.* Stoke: Trentham.

McVeigh, R. (1995) Cherishing the children of the nation unequally: sectarianism in Ireland, in: P. Clancy, S. Drudy, K. Lynch and L. O'Dowd (Eds.) *Irish Society: sociological perspectives.* Dublin: IPA.

McVeigh, R. (1998) Is sectarianism racism? Theorising the racism/sectarianism interface, in: D. Miller (Ed.) *Rethinking Northern Ireland.* Harlow: Addison Wesley Longman.

Rodley, N. (2001) *A Bill of Rights for Northern Ireland: some international lessons.* Lecture to Committee on the Administration of Justice, Malone Lodge, Belfast, 31 May.

Smyth, M., and Moore, R. (1995) Researching Sectarianism. http://www.ccruni.gov. uk/research/temple/confer1.htm (accessed 30.01.04).

Sutton, M. (2003) Sutton Index of Deaths. http://cain.ulst.ac.uk/sutton/ (accessed: 29.03.04).

Tajfel, H., and Turner, J.C. (1979) An integrative theory of intergroup conflict, in: W.G. Austin and S. Worchel (Eds.) *The Social Psychology of Intergroup Relations.* Monterey, California: Brooks/Cole.

Trew, K. (1986) Catholic-Protestant contact in Northern Ireland, in: M. Hewstone and R. Brown (Eds.) *Contact and Conflict in Intergroup Encounters.* Oxford: Basil Blackstaff.

United Nations Commission on Human Rights (2004) *Follow-up to the United Nations Decade for Human Rights Education.* Resolution 2004/71. 21 April. www. ohchr.org

Notes

1   Article 5 of the Race Relations (NI) Order defines a 'racial group' as 'a group of persons defined by reference to colour, race, nationality or ethnic or national origins'. This definition and use of the term 'race' generally are problematic as they imply biological connotations that are misleading and fail to capture the social and cultural differences that exist between groups, which are not innate. See Connolly (2002a).

2   DENI commissioned the UNESCO Centre at the University of Ulster to carry out the evaluation. We are grateful for the competent research assistance provided by Claire Peters (University of Ulster) and Mary Kelly (Marlborough College, USA).

3   Nine schools were classified as secondary schools, four as grammar schools, two as integrated schools, and one was categorised as a special needs school.

4   Standardised instructions for questionnaire completion and all questions were read aloud. Students ticked the appropriate responses on an answer sheet, in order to accommodate those with lower literacy levels. They provided their date of birth and the number of the flat or house they lived in, to allow matching of pre- and post-tests without compromising anonymity of respondents.

5   Teacher interviews were conducted in the school and those for the project co-ordinator and project officers at the university. Interviews ranged from twenty-five minutes to over one hour in length and were recorded for transcription.

6   McNemar test for dependent samples and paired sample t-tests.

5

Citizenship education in the Republic of Ireland

Colm Ó Cuanacháin

Context

I reland, at the beginning of the 21st century, is experiencing a period of considerable change and some uncertainties. The economy is booming, with an average annual growth in Gross National Product of 9.3 per cent over the last decade. Un-employment has fallen from 17.4 per cent in 1986 to 3.9 per cent at the end of 2000. The peace process continues to grind along a slow but steady path. Yet Irish society is facing real challenges, and life for many feels less satisfying. Arguably, it is citizenship, and the values that underpin it, that are in crisis. As Ireland emerges from its recent history of deep and lingering sec-tarianism, the country faces growing challenges relating to racism, crime, and social exclusion. Economic growth coexists with social and civic decline, as Ireland and its people slide backwards across a range of key social indicators. The develop-ment of racist attitudes and behaviour are indicative of the problems facing Irish society.

Ireland's recent economic success is associated with an unsur-prising yet unprecedented change in social demographics. The numbers of migrant workers, asylum seekers and refugees settling in Ireland continue to grow. By 2003 there were 277,600 foreign born people resident in Ireland of whom 118,700, or 3 per cent of the total population, were born outside the European Union (EU) (Central Statistics Office, 2003). This represents a marked increase over previous years. At the same time, racism is gaining strength. The Equality Authority reported that in 2003 race discrimination overtook gender discrimination in the number of cases instigated under the Employment Equality Act 1998; one third of all cases cited race-related grounds (Crowley, 2003). 62 per cent of young people (15-24 years) believe that the Irish are becoming more racist (*Irish Times*/MRBI, 2003). Institutional racism is also a problem: a judge, speaking in a district court in February 2003, warned that 'coloured' people may soon be banned from shopping centres as a consequence of shoplifting incidents (NCCRI, 2003: 4). When people from ethnic minorities living in Ireland were asked about their experiences, 80 per cent believed racism to be a serious problem. Nine out of ten black people questioned said they had experienced racism (FAQ Research, 2001).

Racism is not a new phenomenon in Ireland. The appalling treatment of Travellers is sad testimony to that fact (O'Connell, 2002). Central to debates on discrimination and the promotion of citizenship in Ireland are nationalism and the festering legacy of sectarianism that has been linked to it for over 400 years of Irish history:

> Irish nationalism has meant the hegemony of a Catholic, 'white', sedentary collectivity over both state and society, without reference to the truly multi-ethnic nature of Irish society. (Lentin, 2002: 163)

However, the rise in racism is but one dimension to the developing social chassis. The gap between the richest and the poorest citizens in Ireland is now the biggest of any EU country (SVP, 2003). During the course of the recent economic boom, levels of relative poverty actually increased. In 1994, 17.4 per cent of the population were living on less than half the average income. This had risen to 20.9 per cent by the year 2000 (O'Toole, 2003: 63). In 1999, 5,234 persons were recorded as homeless, twice as many as in 1996 (Simon Community, 2003). Serious crime increased by 23 per cent in 2002 alone (Garda, 2003: 86).

There are tensions across economic, social, cultural, civil and political life that make it difficult for the country as a whole to reap the full social rewards from the recent boom. The clear challenge is to ensure that people can embrace economic development in a framework informed by justice, peace, equality, non-discrimination and inclusion. Education is central in ensuring such a framework for citizenship. While much progress has been made in the areas of policy and curricula, training and resources also need to be made available so that teachers are able to implement policies in the classroom.

Policy

The Irish education system is undergoing its most significant review in 150 years. Over the past decade the Department of Education and Science (DES) has led in a series of innovations, including a National Convention on Education 1993, the 1995 White Paper *Charting Our Education Future,* the Education Act 1998 and revised curricula across all levels. Elements of education for citizenship permeate the new-look education system. *Charting our Educational Future* sets out the government's obligations to promote and protect fundamental human rights (Government of Ireland, 1995: 3-4). The Education Act 1998 placed democratic school systems and structures on a statutory footing for the first time. It requires school boards to provide 'information to students and student councils' about school matters (Government of Ireland, 1998a: 26). The participative and shared approach to learning implicit in any citizenship education programme is now underpinned in law. The revised primary school curriculum lists a set of issues identified through review processes, including 'pluralism, respect for diversity and the importance of tolerance'. It highlights 'the function of the curriculum in contributing to equality and fairness of access to education' (Government of Ireland, 1999a: 9). These examples indicate how citizenship studies based on human rights principles are now recognised as a fundamental aspect of Irish education.

Although the educational policy framework aims to promote citizenship, it is important to remember that discrimination is often so pervasive, historically reinforced and commonplace that even those experiencing it may not be fully aware of how it operates (Taran and Gachter, 2003). An education system that seeks to promote active citizenship needs to be located within a broader society that welcomes positive and participative citizenship. Currently, there is no integrated government educational or social policy framework on citizenship. The limited initiatives relating to ethnic minorities, antiracism and discrimination are generally uncoordinated. The resultant contradictions and inadequacies are stark and are to be found across all policy areas. So, for example, there is as yet no official acknowledgement of institutional racism. Policies to tackle institutional racism in education and to encourage recruitment of teachers from ethnic minority communities are urgently needed. Schools need guidelines and procedures to support them in responding to diversity, for example, in the appointment of language assistants for children whose first language is not English. The government has accepted that the current law is inadequate in addressing racially motivated crime, but there is no system for reporting and recording such crimes, and further legislation is needed. These examples highlight some of the gaps that need to be addressed in the development of a comprehensive policy framework to promote and foster active citizenship in Ireland.

Curriculum

The primary (4-12 years) and post primary junior cycle (12-15 years) curricula have been revised considerably over recent years, while the post primary senior cycle (15-18 years) programme is being revamped at the time of writing. This review has been stewarded by the governmental National Council for Curriculum and Assessment (NCCA). The NCCA curriculum reform processes and outputs have been very encouraging for educators dedicated to participative learning and citizenship studies. The NCCA chief executive, Dr Anne Looney, clearly understands the importance of human rights education:

> [T]he stratification of knowledge within the curriculum creates abstractions and compartmentalisation which inevitably favour

certain sectors of the population. Add to this an assessment system which supports this stratification of knowledge, and curriculum becomes not a site for human rights education but a source of human rights concern. Equality is not possible when knowledge is this stratified. (Looney, 2000: 20)

The NCCA has consistently sought to design curricula through comprehensive, in-depth consultation processes with stakeholders, generating content that is integrated and a holistic structure where the methodological, management and structural dimensions to schooling are interdependent. Lister (1984) has informed an approach to education *in, for* and *through* rights that has found its way into some aspects of the revised Irish curricula. This approach has been developed in 'about-through-for' dimensions to citizenship education (Davies, 2000: 10). Any Irish educator seeking to implement this approach in the classroom would find ample scope in the current curricula.

Primary (Age 4 – 12)

The revised primary school curriculum includes a specific aim 'to enable children to develop a respect for cultural difference, an appreciation of civic responsibility, and an understanding of the social dimension of life, past and present' (Government of Ireland, 1999a: 34). The revised curriculum includes Social Personal and Health Education (SPHE) as the core subject area through which citizenship is to be driven in the primary school. SPHE provides opportunities to help the child become 'an active and responsible citizen' through a 'framework of values, attitudes, understanding and skills' (Government of Ireland, 1999b: 2). It includes a unit where children 'learn about individual and group rights and responsibilities, particularly in the context of their school and local community' (Government of Ireland, 1999b: 17).

The revised curriculum was introduced on a phased basis, and SPHE came on stream in 2003/2004. The syllabus envisages that children will experience SPHE through a positive school climate. The SPHE curriculum fosters in children respect for their own dignity and that of others and promotes a healthy lifestyle and a commitment to the democratic process (NCCA, 1998: 7). Teachers involved in the Curriculum Committee that drafted the SPHE programme characterised it as follows:

> SPHE is concerned with a number of interrelated human quali-
> ties... These qualities are life-enhancing, prosocial, promote a
> healthy lifestyle, are respectful of human dignity and diversity and
> foster the democratic way of life. As children develop these quali-
> ties they are given a foundation of values, attitudes, skills and
> understandings about themselves, other people and the society in
> which they live. (Kavanagh and Sheils, 1997: 71)

Post-Primary Junior Cycle (Age 12 – 15)

The DES introduced a new course to the junior cycle of secondary schools in September 1996 following a nationwide pilot
project. The course, entitled Civic, Social and Political Education (CSPE), 'is a course in citizenship, based on human rights
and social responsibilities [that] aims to develop active citizens'
(Government of Ireland, 1998b: 5). Its aim is 'to enable and empower students to become participative, aware and responsible
citizens' (CDU, 2002: 5).

The programme covers four units: the individual and citizenship; the community; the State – Ireland; and Ireland and the
World. It is envisaged that teachers will adopt a thematic
approach to the subject and explore specific given themes, including human rights, across all of the units:

> Within these broadly defined units teachers have much scope and
> flexibility to select and deal with specific issues such as gender
> equity, racism, interculturalism, work and unemployment, poverty,
> homelessness and the environment. (Osler and Vincent 2002: 84)

CSPE is assessed at the end of a three-year study programme on
the basis of a written exam (40 per cent) and an action project
(60 per cent). The projects are based on participation in some
form of civic, social or political actions at school or community
level (Hammond *et al.*, 2001: 5).

Having completed the Junior Certificate Examination, post-
primary students generally move on to the Transition Year (TY),
which is a programme that is activity based and aimed at
developing life-skills through use of very different methodo-

logies and curriculum content. TY is seen as an opportunity to reinforce and build upon the main aim of CSPE, to develop active and participatory citizenship in pupils with regard to human rights and social responsibilities. Social justice in action is a central element to the TY programme. Students can opt to work in the local community with a social justice project. Alternatively, the programme can involve a year-long programme of events, talks, and projects on social justice and citizenship.

Post-Primary Senior Cycle (Age 15 –18)

The current leaving certificate curriculum includes citizenship education across a number of subject areas. For example, in the recently launched Home Economics, Social and Scientific syllabus, there are strong elements of citizenship studies, with themes on home, family, environment, and global studies presented in an interdependent framework (Government of Ireland, 2001). Unfortunately, there is no coordination or other attempt at coherence between various subjects.

A number of contributors, notably the Curriculum Development Unit (CDU), are making a strong case for a continuation of a dedicated syllabus on citizenship from junior cycle into the senior cycle (CDU 2000; Hammond, 2002; Ward, 2002). Significantly, the NCCA set out the directions for development of the senior cycle based on feedback received during the consultation process. In addition to envisioning a future where school management, organisation, and school/community linking is more participative and conducive to citizenship learning, the NCCA anticipates that 'short courses in politics and society, media studies, social, personal and health education, and European and global studies' will be part of the programme (NCCA, 2003: 6).

Disappointingly, the comprehensive consultations conducted as part of curriculum review have not generated educational policies or strategies that are inclusive of new ethnic minorities in Ireland. While this unsatisfactory situation is not unique to Ireland (Osler and Starkey, 2001) the opportunity now exists within the revised senior cycle curricula to redress this.

Teacher Training

Citizenship education is not a formal or compulsory element of pre-service teacher training at either primary or post-primary level. The Equality Authority (2003: 11-12) outlines the challenges facing Irish schools, including the accommodation of diversity and in helping children develop ideas and values. It also stresses the role of schools in helping students to understand the causes of inequality and empowering them to challenge these inequalities. The National Plan Against Racism (NPAR) Steering Group (2003) identified the need to build an intercultural and antiracism dimension to education and training policy in Ireland. It identified this area of education as a priority for the government, advocating a whole school approach to include school management, policies, planning and evaluation. Lack of training in intercultural and antiracism education was also highlighted as a concern by the Irish National Teacher's Organisation (INTO, 1998: 24, 35-37).

In its First National Report to the UN Committee on the Elimination of Racial Discrimination, the Irish Government is silent on the preparation of teachers in antiracism and interculturalism. In fact, the only reference to teacher training is a general statement reporting that at primary level 'the new curricula are supported by in-service training, teacher guidelines, and full-time staff development teams' (Government of Ireland: 2004: 161).

Primary Level

In-service training in SPHE is supported by a team of ten trainers. The trainers are available to schools across the country and their role is to provide training and mentoring services for over 20,000 teachers across some 3,200 primary schools. This team is responsible for supporting the entire SPHE programme, and not just citizenship. This level of support is inadequate, particularly as this is a new subject and therefore a new demand on teachers. The introduction of the new SPHE curriculum to all schools from 2003 means that the teacher training colleges will now provide pre-service citizenship studies training. Additionally, the Development and Intercultural Education

(DICE) project, launched in 2003, aims to incorporate development and intercultural education into primary initial teacher training. The DES facilitates a programme of optional summer in-service courses at both primary and post-primary levels, which are usually organised by independent trainers or organisations and include courses in citizenship studies.

Post-primary Level

Post-primary teachers receive pre-service training through the Higher Diploma in Education, offered in a number of Irish universities. In response to the introduction of the CSPE and TY programmes at post-primary level, these courses now include basic elective modules in citizenship studies.

The DES established the Second Level Support Service (SLSS) to oversee staff development and curriculum innovation at post-primary level. SLSS provides support for both the TY and CSPE programmes. As at primary level, there are serious concerns about the lack of resources for in-service training at post-primary level (Drudy and Coolahan, 2002). This has implications for all subjects and is particularly acute at a time when new curricula are being introduced.

Lack of commitment to citizenship studies training is also found in programmes that fall outside the remit of the DES. The Irish Government has cut the financial allocation to a number of key State bodies working to promote citizenship, in areas such as antiracism education and equality. Resources for the Government's antiracism awareness campaigning body, Know Racism, were cut by 63 per cent in 2003 and a further 76 per cent in 2004. Similarly, the Equality Authority experienced a 5 per cent budget cut in 2003 and a further 2.5 per cent in 2004 (Coulter, 2003).

The Irish Human Rights Commission has observed that:

> Much excellent work in teaching tolerance and inclusivity is being done in schools, but more funding is needed. Given the gravity and urgency of the issue, a major effort needs to be put in to mainstreaming human rights and antiracist education and awareness training in all schools and third level colleges through a broad range of subjects right across the curriculum. (HRC, 2002: 15)

Resources

While the DES has succeeded in framing a policy and curriculum base that provides for citizenship studies, the lack of training, support and resources appears to be restricting the emergence of best practice and energetic implementation at classroom level. Teachers' organisations and professional bodies are, nevertheless, spearheading a number of successful classroom initiatives. Of course these programmes would not be happening at all but for the solid educational context provided by DES, but much more would be achieved if government invested as much in practice as it has in policy. This lacuna is particularly acute in the area of classroom resources.

The *Intercultural Guidelines for Schools*, produced by the Irish National Teachers' Organisation (INTO, 2002) and distributed to all primary schools, are a good example of the positive contribution of non-governmental organisations (NGOs) in developing resources. The guidelines set out a robust and holistic framework for a whole-school approach to interculturalism and citizenship in Irish primary schools. They cover every aspect of school life from enrolment policy to inclusive strategies for parents, from whole-school approaches to a sample school charter.

Some other good examples of resources produced by NGOs with and for teachers include:

■ The *World in the Classroom* (Ruane *et al.*, 1999) and 80:20 – development in an unequal world (80 : 20, 2002).

■ *Lift Off* (Cross Border Primary Human Rights Education Initiative, 2003) a human rights education resource for primary schools, based on a cross-border initiative that was piloted in twenty schools and which is being introduced to all primary schools across Ireland, north and south.

■ the widely used *All Different All Equal* (DEFY, 1994) an anti-racism education resource and *An Activity Pack for Schools and Youth Workers* (NCCRI, 2001), a short and basic manual on antiracism education.

■ The *Citizenship Development Programme* is a module delivered in TY in the Republic of Ireland and in Year 13 in
Northern Ireland. It is linked to the *Human Rights, Conflict
and Dialogue Programme*, which offers post-primary senior
cycle students in participating schools the opportunity to
explore human rights themes. Both projects are co-
ordinated by St Angela's College of Education, as part of
their Transform Conflict initiative.

These resources have common features including the use of inclusive and participative methodologies, whole-school approaches, and a child-centred structure, all of which are critical
to citizenship education.

The dearth of government funding in this area is undermining
the piloting, development and provision of high-quality teaching resources for use in schools. At least four significant
organisations working to provide training and resources for
teachers in aspects of citizenship studies have closed over the
past two years due to funding constraints.

Citizenship education also needs to be advanced through non-
formal channels. Indeed it is critical that young adults, excluded
from school and already feeling a sense of marginalisation, be
given the opportunities to develop the skills and attitudes required for active citizenship. One World Week (or Global Education Week as it known in a number of European countries) is
celebrated annually in Ireland with the production of educational packs on global issues that are circulated to youth groups
and non-formal educational organisations and networks. The
programme is promoted by an advisory group, a network of
partners, and a training programme. In 2003, for example, the
theme related to conflict and sought to promote 'a knowledge of
and respect for human dignity, with its associated rights and
duties' (Sheehan, 2003).

Gaelscoil: a case study

A number of individual teachers and some schools are emerging as examples of best practice in citizenship studies. One such
initiative is in *Gaelscoil,* a multi-denominational, co-educa-

tional primary school located in a city suburb (Ruane, *et al.*, 1999). The Irish curricula are devised in a manner that affords schools a wide degree of autonomy in terms of the education programme they implement, working within the broad DES framework. Taking advantage of this, the school decided to specialise in human rights education. A policy and programme on human rights education were developed following consultative processes involving the staff, the board of management, and children. Implementation began during 1999/2000 as part of an action research project conducted by this author (O'Cuanacháin, 2004). The project, which was monitored, recorded and evaluated as part of the action research process, sought to enable a learning environment in which children would experience human rights and active citizenship first hand: 'For young people to learn about human rights they must experience them and believe in them, as well as know about them' (Osler and Starkey, 1996 : 85).

The human rights education policy generated by the school community identified education for active citizenship as a central aspect of the school ethos. Once devised, the policy was formally included in the school plan, a document required under the Education Act 1998 that sets out the school's policies, structures, procedures, and curriculum. The policy was implemented through a human rights education programme, which was developed specifically for the school with input from the teaching staff and other stakeholders. The programme sought to promote the knowledge, attitudes and skills needed to equip the children to become active, informed and caring citizens. It was an integrated whole school initiative that was taught in all classes and included a number of cross-curricular units and multi-class modules.

Relevant themes and lesson plans for each class were devised in discussion with the class teacher. The content was appropriate to each age level, and was integrated as part of the broader work undertaken in each class. An emphasis was placed on the use of participative methodologies throughout. Steps were taken to organise and manage the school in a human rights framework where discipline, school organisation, relationships, and learning take place in a shared democratic environment. Examples of these mechanisms, which were part of the action-research project, included school assemblies, class contracts, a school declaration, a school court and a school council. Aspects of development education, peace education, citizenship studies, education for democracy, and conflict resolution were all intertwined in the programme and taught within a human rights framework.

A number of obstacles had to be overcome before the action-research project could be implemented. For example, the lack of training available to teachers (pre-service or in-service) had to be addressed through the provision of an elaborate set of teachers' resources and regular staff discussions. This ran deeper than training in content, as methodologies and evaluation techniques also had to be explored with the staff. The initiative required all involved to commit a significant investment of time, particularly in the start-up phase. To be truly experiential the programme had to work at and beyond classroom level, but this proved difficult in practice as coordinating activities with different classes and groupings is not something that school structures are easily equipped to deal with, or used to in practice.

The project was evaluated through interviews, diaries from the teachers, and a longitudinal survey with the children. There was unanimous endorsement and welcome for the human rights education processes introduced to the school, by both the teachers and the pupils. Everybody who contributed to the action research reported that the processes had a positive impact. Teachers felt that the attitudes the process cultivated, and will cultivate through continuous reflective interaction with others, will enable the children to live better in a changing, more intercultural, more diverse, and more challenging society in Ireland and the world. All teachers reported that cooperation and understanding appeared to improve between the children and their classmates, with increased evidence of interest in relationships and communication.

The children said that they enjoyed learning through participation. They eagerly anticipated the next human rights education sessions. They felt that the approaches they had experienced had helped them to see life from a broader perspective, and that it had changed the way they think about certain things. For example, nearly all children consulted after the implementation phase felt that the human rights education programme had contributed to stemming bullying and unfair treatment in the school, as the following two quotes from children illustrate:

> It's a good idea to learn about human rights so that we will have a better school.

> It made bullies feel ashamed. It worked on me.

They felt that they knew more about others and understood better the problems faced by other people:

> I learned that you should be aware that other people have rights and not just you, and you should help people to know their rights.

> I learned how important rights are, and that there are many people whose rights are being violated right in front of our noses, and we don't care.

Comments from children suggested that the programme helped many of them to think about the world in a way that they had not in the past.

The research also reflected the difficulties that the staff experienced in developing, launching and implementing this new pedagogical, structural and curriculum approach. The training, the time, and the cultural difficulties were evident throughout and not all teachers reported on implementation with equal levels of satisfaction or success. For example, it was agreed that a school court would be established as one of the mechanisms used to promote the participation of children in the workings of the school, by allowing them to organise their own court every Friday afternoon to adjudicate on some of the transgressions of the code of conduct by peers. The aim was for an increased awareness and understanding of the impact of misbehaviour on victims arising from the debate and consideration of their plight. The children would, it was hoped, develop an increased sense of responsibility associated with being part of the justice system. However, plans to establish the court proved too ambitious. As one teacher explained:

> The main problem was the amount of time needed. We didn't think through the whole-school dimension enough. It has implications that we weren't ready for. The school court is a wonderful concept, but it is an entire project in itself to get it up and running, accepted and understood, by teachers and by the children.

The project demonstrates that a human rights school can thrive in the context of current Irish national curricula and government policy. The integrated approach adopted in the school for the action research project worked, and can work in other schools. However, steps should be taken to bridge the identified gap in the provision of training and support (in-service and pre-service) for teachers seeking to promote participative learning, including in the areas of methodologies, classroom management techniques, planning and evaluation. Additional leadership, support and backing for schools and teachers, including policy guidance, resources and practical direction, need to be provided by the DES. This should include areas such as school management, integrated implementation of the revised curriculum, whole-school approaches and time allocation. Such support is critical if teachers are to feel empowered to fully embrace participative and holistic approaches.

Conclusion

In a recent study conducted for the Irish Department of Foreign Affairs, the youngest age group surveyed (12-24 years) professed to know the least about developing countries. On the other hand, 63 per cent indicated their willingness to learn more about these countries and peoples (Cremin, 2002: 27). What is interesting is the fact that the survey took place six years after the full introduction in Ireland of what is widely regarded as a good curriculum for citizenship studies aimed precisely at the age group surveyed. While the curriculum appears, at face value, to be strong on citizenship, human rights and development, it appears that it may not be having an impact in practice. One message that we must take from this is that the curriculum is not enough. If active citizenship is to thrive, it will require more than a set of subjects framed to provide opportunities for teachers to explore citizenship. It will require training, resources, structural reforms at school level, and a more committed approach to citizenship studies from educators and society as a whole. In this way, the tide of negative social trends in Ireland can be turned.

References

Central Statistics Office (2003) 2002 *Census of Population*, Volume 4, October. Cork: Central Statistics Office.

Coulter, C. (2003) Antiracism body has its budget slashed, *Irish Times*, 14 November.

Cremin, P. (2002) The educational perspective, in: J. A. Weafer (Ed.) *Attitudes Towards Development Cooperation in Ireland*. Dublin: Ireland Aid.

Cross Border Primary Human Rights Education Initiative (2003) *Lift Off: introducing human rights education within the primary curriculum*. Dublin: Cross Border Primary Human Rights Education Initiative.

Crowley, N. (2003) Address at the launch of Anti-Racist Workplace Week 2003 (unpublished). Dublin: Equality Authority.

Curriculum Development Unit (CDU) (2000) *Initial Submission to NCCA on Civic, Social and Political Education within the Established Leaving Certificate*. Dublin: Curriculum Development Unit.

Curriculum Development Unit (CDU) (2002) *Changing Perspectives, Cultural Values, Diversity and Equality in Ireland and the Wider World*. Dublin: Curriculum Development Unit.

Davies, L. (2000) *Citizenship Education and Human Rights Education: key concepts and debates*. London: British Council.

Development Education For Youth (DEFY) (1994) *All Different All Equal*. Dublin: DEFY.

Drudy, S. and Coolahan, J. (2002) In-Career Development for the Teaching Profession: the role of universities and colleges of education. Paper presented to the Advisory Committee on In-Service Programmes for Teachers at Second Level.

Equality Authority (2003) *Schools and the Equal Status Act*. Dublin: Equality Authority.

FAQ Research (2001) *Racism in Ireland: the views of black and ethnic minorities*. Dublin: Amnesty International Irish Section.

Garda (2003) *Garda Siochána Annual Report 2002*. Dublin: An Garda Siochána.

Government of Ireland (1995) *Charting our Education Future – White Paper on Education*. Dublin: The Stationary Office.

Government of Ireland (1998a) *Education Act*. Dublin: The Stationary Office.

Government of Ireland (1998b) *Civic, Social and Political Education – guidelines for teachers*. Dublin: Department of Education and Science.

Government of Ireland (1999a) *Primary School Curriculum*. Dublin: Department of Education and Science.

Government of Ireland (1999b) *Social, Personal and Health Education – Teacher Guidelines*. Dublin: Department of Education and Science.

Government of Ireland (2001) *Leaving Certificate Home Economics, Social and Scientific Syllabus*. Dublin: Department of Education and Science.

Government of Ireland (2004) *First National Report to the UN Committee on the Elimination of Racial Discrimination*. Dublin: The Stationary Office.

Hammond, J. (2002) Why Social and Political Education at Senior Cycle? in: *Combat Poverty Agency and Curriculum Development Unit . Charting the Future: social and political education in the senior cycle of post-primary schools*. Dublin: Curriculum Development Unit.

Hammond, J., Looney, A., and McCarthy, S. (2001) Education for Democratic Citizenship: the development of EDC policy in the Republic of Ireland at lower post-primary level. Strasbourg: Paper presented at the Council for Cultural Cooperation, 31 May.

Human Rights Commission (HRC) (2002) *Submission to the National Action Plan Against Racism*. Dublin: Human Rights Commission.

Irish National Teachers Organisation (INTO) (1998) *The Challenge of Diversity: education support for ethnic minority children*. Dublin: INTO.

Irish National Teachers Organisation (INTO) (2002) *Intercultural Guidelines for Schools*. Dublin: INTO.

Irish Times/MRBI (2003) Youth Poll. 20 September.

Kavanagh, N. and Sheils, S. (1997) *Social, Personal and Health Education: curriculum change*. Dublin: INTO.

Lentin, R. (2002) 'Who ever heard of an Irish Jew?' The intersection of 'Irishness' and 'Jewishness', in: R. Lentin and R. McVeigh (Eds.) *Racism and Antiracism in Ireland*. Belfast: Beyond the Pale.

Lister, I. (1984) *Teaching and Learning about Human Rights*. Strasbourg: Council of Europe, School Education Division.

Looney, A. (2000) Human rights education: imagination and curriculum, in: K. O'Shea, B. Gill and A. Clifford (Eds.) *Towards an Integrated Approach to Human Rights Education*. Dublin: Curriculum Development Unit.

National Consultative Committee on Racism and Interculturalism (NCCRI) (2001) *An Activity Pack for Schools and Youth Workers*. Dublin: NCCRI.

National Consultative Committee on Racism and Interculturalism (NCCRI) (2003) *Reported Incidents Related to Racism, November 2002 – April 2003*. Dublin: NCCRI.

National Council for Curriculum and Assessment (NCCA) (1998) *Comhairle, Primary School Curriculum Preview*. Dublin: NCCA.

National Council for Curriculum and Assessment (NCCA) (2003) *Directions for Development*. Dublin: NCCA.

National Plan Against Racism (NPAR) (2003) *A Summary of the Outcomes of the Consultative Process and a Proposed Framework for the National Action Plan Against Racism*. Dublin: The Stationary Office.

O'Connell, J. (2002) Travellers in Ireland: an examination of discrimination and racism, in: R. Lentin and R. McVeigh (Eds.) *Racism and Antiracism in Ireland*. Belfast: Beyond the Pale.

O'Cuanacháin, C. (2004) Human Rights Education in an Irish Primary School. Unpublished PhD thesis, University of Leicester.

Osler, A., and Starkey, H. (1996) *Teacher Education and Human Rights.* London: David Fulton.

Osler, A., and Starkey, H. (2001) Citizenship education and national identities in France and England: inclusive or exclusive? *Oxford Review of Education*, 27 (2): 287-305.

Osler, A., and Vincent, K. (2002) *Citizenship and the Challenge of Global Education.* Stoke: Trentham.

O'Toole, F. (2003) *After the Ball.* Dublin: Tasc at New Island.

Ruane, B., Horgan, K. and Cremin, P. (1999) *The World in the Classroom: development education in the primary curriculum.* Limerick: Curriculum Development Unit, Mary Immaculate College of Education.

Sheehan, J. (2003) *Peace by Piece.* Dublin: One World Week.

Simon Community (2003) *It's Hard to Understand why People who are Homeless are still Denied the Chance of a Decent Home: Simon Community Annual Report 2002/ 2003.* Dublin: Simon Community.

Society of Saint Vincent de Paul (SVP) (2003) *Annual Report of the Society of Saint Vincent de Paul 2003.* Dublin: SVP.

Taran, P. and Gachter, A. (2003) *Achieving Equality in an Intercultural Workplace: an agenda for action.* Dublin: Equality Authority.

Ward, E. (2002), *Citizenship Studies: a curricular proposal for social and political education in the Leaving Certificate (Established).* Dublin: Curriculum Development Unit.

80:20 (2002) 80:20 *Development in An Unequal World.* Dublin: 80: 20.

PART TWO
STUDENTS, TEACHERS AND
HUMAN RIGHTS

6

'You did the best you can': history, citizenship and moral dilemmas

Hilary Claire

Histstory is closely linked to citizenship education – both through its content and its processes. So, for example, how power has been exercised or resisted in different civilizations, or specific campaigns challenging injustice, such as the emancipation, suffrage or civil rights campaigns, all provide content for both history and citizenship education. The fundamental historical skills of analysing and interpreting evidence, recognising propaganda or developing convincing, evidence-based explanations are all relevant to citizenship education. In one area of citizenship, however – social and moral development – the links with history have not been widely explored, even though history has traditionally been associated with young people's moral development and the choice of content is often justified in these terms.

This chapter reports on research with primary-aged children in inner city schools, from the many communities living in London today. The research drew on a number of historical narratives which challenged the children to consider 'the right

thing to do'. I used story, direct questioning and role-play techniques, to explore their responses to moral dilemmas involving
human rights, equality and social justice and their understanding of some social and moral aspects of choice.

Rights, responsibilities and ethics

The citizenship curriculum for school students acknowledges
that citizens can neither understand nor exercise their rights
and responsibilities in a moral vacuum; hence social and moral
education is a strand in the primary citizenship guidance, and
in the statutory secondary curriculum (see QCA, 1998 and
1999). In a democracy, a citizen needs not only to develop a coherent set of values which are in tune with social justice, but
also a personal ethic which will underpin the daily choices
which contribute to equitable and effective personal relationships. In addition, as I discuss in Claire (2001), in the spirit of
feminist moral philosophy (Noddings, 1986; Larrabee 1993),
humane, people-centred ethical codes should be informed by
care and compassion, and not just by utilitarianism or overarching precepts about right and wrong (deontology). Care and
compassion are, in my view, not replacements for utilitarianism
and deontology, but provide ethical principles for social justice
– lenses through which one can evaluate one's attitudes and
actions, their motives and consequences. The research on
which I report in this chapter focused on moral choices relevant
to human rights, social justice and equality. All were con-
textualised in situations requiring not just a willingness and
ability to empathise with others' moral dilemmas and personal
difficulties, but also an on-going review of moral choices in the
light of risks and consequences for a variety of people, not just
oneself. For these reasons, the research processes provide a
possible vehicle for developing more mature understandings
and responses.

Historical significance

In the history national curriculum for England, children at both
Key Stage 1 (5 to 7-year-olds) and Key Stage 2 (7 to 11-year-olds)
are required to study significant individuals as well as signi-

ficant events and issues. A great many people have been significant for the evil they have done rather than the good but, con-
ventionally in primary school, teachers concentrate on people
who, in the retrospective judgement of history, have tried to
contribute to a more socially just world. Teachers, enjoined to
consider 'historical significance' in their choice of individuals
and content, are given no guidance about the meaning of the
concept. This is not only unhelpful for interpreting the statutory
orders for history, and for teaching the history effectively, but
also means an opportunity is lost to link history to children's
education in citizenship. Attribution of historical significance
occurs with hindsight and concentration on outcomes. Learning to evaluate significance is an important skill, enabling
students to look beyond intentions (however benign) towards
consequences, whether intended, contingent or untoward.
Through history students learn to consider the consequences
not just for one individual actor or group, but from a variety of
perspectives and over short, medium or long periods. If
addressed with appropriate regard for multi-causality and complexity of outcomes, the study of significance challenges
simplistic, quick-fix notions and mono-dimensional perspectives on change.

With respect to citizenship education, there is another aspect to
the evaluation of significance. This relates to students' developing ethics and values, since significance itself is not value free.
So inviting students to consider significance can contribute to
their ability to consider the proposals and programmes on offer,
not just in terms of what might be, but also with an eye for
possible knock-on or side effects.

An important aspect of significance relates to the chain of consequences, including changed or hardened attitudes, expectations or fears resulting from some event or movement. It is a
truism that citizens, trying to make sense of the present, but
also considering possibilities for the future, need to understand
their society's past. Students' analytic thinking and ability to
make connections cannot be taken for granted.

A study in the United States about students' ability to evaluate the significance of quite recent events revealed that it is unwise to assume that they will either know about or appreciate the chaining of events and attitudes which underpin current attitudes and actions (Levstick, 2000). For instance, while adolescent American students thought that the Vietnam War had significance for veterans, they did not appreciate its part in challenging attitudes to authority or to American military intervention, or how it contributed to civil rights. Levstick concluded that if teachers want children to make connections between history and contemporary circumstances, they themselves needed to take a meta-cognitive approach and to model understanding about causal chains and current significance. It is not enough to leave the transference of ideas and connections to chance.

The relevance to this chapter is twofold. First, if children are to develop their powers of social and moral reasoning through history, to the benefit of citizenship, then it will not be enough for teachers to leave the discussion with matters in the past. They will need to help their students appreciate the contemporary relevance. Children may do this in part for themselves, drawing on personal contemporary knowledge, but teachers will also have to help them map the connections.

Dilemmas, history and ethical thinking
Developing an ethical framework within which value judgements and choices about our society and our own actions can be made does not happen in a content free zone. Typically, in primary school, such work is confined to literature and religious education, with occasional forays into geography. However, emphasis in the history curriculum on the lives and contributions of significant individuals can and should take us straight to the heart of ethics. Many significant people have made choices, often going against tradition, taking risks, and accepting or even choosing physical and social hardship and self-sacrifice. To my knowledge, the potential of history to provide real life, authentic dilemmas in which children are asked to grapple with choices in imperfect contexts has not been ex-

ploited, possibly because hindsight about what actually happened is thought to close down the kind of hypothetical, exploratory thinking about consequences which ethical thinking entails. Yet opportunities exist for children to try to understand and get into other people's skins, and also to develop their personal codes of morality, albeit in contexts which are from another time and place.

The work which I describe in this chapter requires a strong commitment to hypothetical moral thinking. It involves being explicit with children that one is not really trying to recreate the lives and thought of people in the past, but working with the dilemmas that they really faced in their time, facilitated or constrained by the physical and material conditions which they experienced. Not all primary teachers, and few children, will find it easy to work with empathy, role-play and the demands of 'imagining you are so-and-so' and retain a sense of the uniqueness of specific peoples, periods and places. If teachers and children do not relapse into ahistoricity, and pay careful attention to the historical detail, this work can enhance the study of history itself. To achieve this, the teacher at least must have done her homework!

Research method

In the mid-1990s, as part of research into children's thinking and understanding, I worked with 22 pairs of primary aged children, aged between 7-11 years, from two inner-London schools. As well as general interviews about their lives, which are reported in *Not Aliens* (Claire, 2001), all the children worked with me on a series of history stories. The research was designed to give children opportunities to discuss authentic moral dilemmas and conflicts which connected to contemporary controversial issues. In this case, the decision about significance was mine, and not opened up to discussion with the children – though it might have been. I was not interested in whether the children understood the historical significance of the events, but how they engaged with the moral dilemmas. Since I also had the transcripts about their personal concerns, I was interested in making links between their responses to the history stories and their personal lives, if these emerged. Since I was not their teacher, I did not follow up the interviews with curriculum work which would have made the connections with contemporary citizenship issues that I have advocated above.

From the mass of transcripts, I have selected four pairs of children (see Figure 1). They are neither typical nor exceptional. They did not necessarily provide fuller or more interesting transcripts than other pairs, but exemplify the ways that the children tackled the issues, and how they construed the ethical problems. Of necessity, the extracts chosen are very short.

The children came to me in self-selected pairs. All were already familiar with me through the personal interviews we had conducted earlier.[1] Of the eight children, only Harriet and Emily came from middle-class families (using where they lived and

Figure 6.1: Background information on the four pairs of children

Names	Gender	Age	Background/heritage
Simon	Boys	11 years	Mixed heritage – Caribbean /white English parents
Ibrahim	Year 6		Born in Bangladesh, both parents Bangladeshi; lived in England for 6 years
Cherise	Girls Year 6	10 years	English born; both parents Caribbean; living with mother alone
Francesca			English born; mixed heritage, parents: mother – black Zimbabwean/white English mixed heritage; father – Caribbean
Harriet	Girls Year 4	9 years	English born, white; mother ex-South African, father English
Emily			English born; white, both parents English
Toyin	Girls Year 4	8 years	English born; both parents Nigerian
Farzana			English born; Bangladeshi parents

parents' profession/work as the criteria). In both schools I worked in a private room using a tape recorder. The history interviews were normally completed in one session.

The history stories: themes and issues

The research was based on five stories, each dealing with an episode in the life of a person of significance or dealing with significant issues. The characters selected were Nelson Mandela; Allen Jay, an 11-year-old white Quaker boy involved in the Underground Railroad;[2] Miep Gies, the Dutch woman who helped keep Anne Frank and her family alive for the two years that they were in hiding from the Nazis in Amsterdam;[3] Cissie Foley, a young late nineteenth century trade unionist and suffragist from Blackburn (Foley, 1973); and Christa Wolf, a twentieth century German writer, who was educated in the Nazi era and was a member of the Hitler Youth. As an adult, Wolf (1983) has cast a highly critical investigative eye on her own past and that of her contemporaries.[4]

The inclusion of Cissie Foley's story allowed me to address issues of workers' rights, family loyalties, gender-defined roles and feminism. Christa Wolf's story is about the importance of historical truth and whether it is better to forget the past in the interests of comfort, or risk the painful acknowledgement of collusion and guilt that honesty entails. In this chapter, I confine myself to discussion of the first three stories – Mandela, Allen Jay and Miep Gies.

In terms of significance and moral choices, these three stories were chosen because they represent critical moments in the struggle against racism. Racism remains a poison in our political system, a reality in the lives of children in inner-city schools. The stories take place at moments of heightened concern and action about issues of race, responsibility, human rights and social justice, forced by peculiar and extreme contexts. I was interested in how children would interpret 'the right thing to do' in these extreme situations. The questions I wished to explore included:

■ What criteria would children use in determining 'the right thing to do'?

■ How do they make their judgements?

■ To what extent can drama techniques and dialogue enable children to develop moral thinking?

■ What is the potential of this approach in exploring and developing children's moral thinking?

■ What are the implications for children's social and moral development, and their understanding of rights and responsibilities in the context of the antiracist agenda of citizenship education?

The likelihood of any child actually being in the position of any of the protagonists is just as remote as their needing to decide whether to steal a drug for a sick wife (the famous Hans story, used by Lawrence Kohlberg to categorise stages of moral development). This work on the history stories was not intended to set up hierarchies of moral development, nor to provide children with a blueprint for future decision-making. The intention was to explore how history might be used in order to give children experience in tackling serious, authentic moral issues. These are issues about which they may well be required to have a viewpoint, as local, national or international citizens, at some point. As citizens we may not be asked to hide a refugee, or take up arms against a repressive state, but we certainly are required to evaluate the actions of our government in issues precisely like this. To do this we need not only information about the circumstances, but also a developed moral position which we use to think through the values at stake, and the likely consequences of action, or inaction.

The children and the stories
I started by asking whether the children knew anything about the main character. Only Mandela was known, though several children were confused about who he was, and only Harriet knew where he came from. This was at a time when Mandela was actually visiting Britain and meeting the Queen!

I had written out each story, so that I would present them consistently, and went through them, stopping as often as needed to ask children if they understood, or if there was anything they wanted explained. Their questions (which I do not have space to discuss here) are extremely revealing, indicating not only areas of difficulty in understanding, but where their interests lay. There were several factual questions, some to elucidate an element of the story, some to provide contextual information. For example, I needed to explain to many of the children some of the specific details of apartheid in South Africa, which some confused with slavery. Some – not necessarily the younger children – were confused by figures of speech such as Underground Railroad. Beyond this, knowing that the stories were true, the majority of children asked questions about the protagonists' families, and about relationships between children and adults, for example, who Mandela's children went to live with after he and Winnie divorced.

The stories, which I told in the present tense, though making clear that they had happened in the past, all contain several moments of choice. Before going on to what actually happened, I stopped at these points and asked the children what they would do, encouraging them to consider the various conflicting emotions, possibilities and implications. They could ask questions to clarify anything they needed to know in trying to decide. Sometimes we used role-play in which I took the part of someone in the story, and asked them take the role of other characters. Sometimes I played devil's advocate and the children had to argue their case against me. Then we continued with the story until we reached the next decision point.

This research method aimed to facilitate the children's engagement and interpretation of issues and to exploit collaborative discussion – even argument – with their friend as well as with me. On many occasions I simply sat back as the children argued out their views. One virtue of this method is that it is transferable from the research setting into the classroom, and simply requires the teacher to set up the narratives embodying dilemmas and moral choices, in line with their particular citizenship concerns, from the period/person in history that the children are studying.

Mandela's story

I asked the children to imagine they were living in South Africa in 1960, shortly after the Sharpeville massacre[5]. They should imagine they were one of Mandela's young children. He comes home one evening saying that he has decided there is no more point in peaceful protest. He will be the leader of the armed struggle and this means he has to go into hiding. What would they say to their father? After they had discussed what they would feel and want to say as the children of Mandela, I asked them to imagine they were Winnie, his wife. What would they say in this role?

Issues to explore

■ Under what conditions might armed struggle, for instance against apartheid, be justified?

■ How did children feel about possible conflicts between leading a resistance movement to achieve change and the responsibilities of a father towards his children/wife?

■ Did they perceive an adult wife's viewpoint differently from a child's (i.e. did they differentiate between the parental responsibilities and priorities of the mother and father, and the position of children)?

Discussion triggers

■ Imagine you were one of Mandela's young children: how would you feel about him getting into something so dangerous?

■ Imagine you were his wife Winnie: what would she be thinking and feeling?

■ You be the children and I'll be Mandela (later Winnie): we're going to have an argument about what I should do and what you want me to do.

Allen Jay and Henry James, the escaped slave

I ask the children to time-travel back to 1842, to the Southern States of America. 11-year-old Allen Jay comes across a runaway slave, who says his name is Henry James. He has been sent to the Jay family through the Underground Railroad. His feet are bleeding, he has been hiding all day in the heat of the fields. Henry asks for Allen's help. The Jays are Quakers, but the penalties from the white Southern community for aiding an escaped slave are extreme. Allen goes to his parents, but Mrs Jay can't leave home because of sick children, and Mr Jay thinks the slave trappers already know him. So they ask Allen to drive the cart to the next 'station' with Henry hidden under some straw.

Issues to explore

■ What sort of personal risks should a family take, in making a stand against an evil like slavery? Does it make any difference if you are white?

■ How far do they see the Jay's religion as placing responsibility on them to help people, or is this irrelevant?

■ What are the responsibilities of parents to their children in situations of grave risk?

■ Speaking as a child, what would you do if called on by your father to help in this situation?

Discussion triggers

■ What should Allen do when Henry approaches him in a field?

■ You are Allen – what is going through your mind? And Henry?

■ What should Mrs Jay advise Allen to do when he goes back home to tell her about Henry? One of you role-play Mrs Jay, the other Allen.

■ Mr Jay wants Allen to take Henry to the next station on the Underground Railroad. This is very dangerous. Should Allen do what his father asks? Role-play Allen and his father.

Miep Gies and the Frank family [8]

I took the children forward in time 100 years from the 1840s, and brought them to Europe. It is the middle of the Second World War. I explained that during the Nazi occupation of Holland, Miep Gies, Otto Frank's former secretary, along with three other helpers, kept the Frank family and the other Jews hiding in the attic for two years before they were betrayed and taken away to the camps. Of the eight people who hid in the attic only Otto survived the camps.

Issues to explore

Rather like the Allen Jay story, this dilemma is about how far a person will take personal risks to save someone else. The difference is that the Frank family are already friends with Miep, whereas Henry James was a stranger to the Jays.

■ Would you risk your own life to help a friend in a situation like the Holocaust?

Discussion triggers

■ Imagine you are Otto, whose daughter Margot has just had the call up, which you think means she will disappear into the camps. What would you say to Miep?

■ What would you say and think if you were Miep?

■ What's going through your mind – as Otto? as Miep?

■ Miep needed the support of her fiancé Jan to help the Franks. Imagine you are Miep talking to Jan.

■ Was it worth the risk, since only Otto Frank survived?

Findings

Under what circumstances might armed struggle be justified?
Mandela's story

Afghanistan, Northern Ireland, the Middle East and former Yugoslavia, Rwanda, Angola, Eritrea, Somalia... Armed struggle and civil war are part of the contemporary world to which children are regularly exposed through television. Some know about such situations first hand or through contact with refugees in their classrooms. Informed attitudes towards events in the wider world are part of citizenship education, but schools are reluctant to acknowledge that primary as well as secondary students are acquiring a variety of ideas beyond the school boundaries. The history curriculum provides opportunities to work with primary students to consider situations of conflict and civil war. Primary school children may better understand contemporary stances by exploring the complex moral dilemmas that resistance or collaboration entail. For example, in the Key Stage 2 primary curriculum they can look critically at non-pacifism in the Second World War or at Iceni support for Boudicaa's rebellion, both of which are typically treated as givens.

In the Mandela story, all the children wanted to explore all possibilities of negotiation fully before they would take up arms. They believed that within a fair system you asked for your rights, among them fair treatment regardless of race, which were then granted by reasonable people. However, if your rights were consistently denied, then 'you should fight for your rights'. Ibrahim was one of the most powerful exponents of racial justice:

> If you don't do anything, how do you know, even today black people might have been slaves.[6] Then what would happen? No one would stand up. They would be afraid of the machine guns. You have to stand up for your colour. Or you're just going to be slaves all of your life. *Ibrahim*

But his friend Simon, a boy of mixed heritage, said he'd leave the country. His justification was not pacifism, but that he would find himself caught in the middle between black and white, implying that he did not conceive that whites could support the cause of justice for blacks.

Farzana asserted: 'People *should* fight if it's for a good cause'. Her partner Toyin's response indicates that she has grasped what apartheid was about:

> You shouldn't fight just because you don't like someone, but he was trying to save his country. Trying to do the right thing... they don't have to do what the government says and they can live where they want and have jobs and live with their children. *Toyin*

In contrast, Emily was concerned that Mandela find a way to achieve the people's rights through putting a good case, emphasising human compassion and empathy with the plight of black people without resorting to violence:

> He wanted people to be able to vote, so he shouldn't get them to fight... they weren't allowed to vote. Mandela was trying to let them, and work out they should be able to vote. [He should have] told them all the things that weren't fair about all the people being separated... and tried to make the government feel sorry for them, 'cos if they felt a bit sorry they could let them go... And it might help, instead of fighting. *Emily*

Emily's liberal position was not generally shared by black children or children of mixed heritage. Her faith in reasonableness and negotiation remained, even when she learned that when Mandela moved to armed struggle it had failed. Her attitude seems appropriate for a democracy but suggests that she had little understanding and experience of situations where empathy and appeals to fair behaviour do not work. In a wider global context in which regular infringements of human rights occurs, despite petitions and pleas, it is important to prepare children to consider what they want to happen when reason breaks down.

Asked what they would have said to Mandela in role as a child or as his wife, when they heard about his decision to engage in armed struggle, the children tended to be supportive of Nelson, but did not necessarily empathise with Winnie. Some children stereotyped a wife as more concerned with the immediate family than with issues of justice. Simon's remarks again suggest how some children draw on personal experience to interpret wider themes. He believed that Winnie would support Nelson because she had an ulterior motive related to having a clandestine affair, and wanted him out of the way, perhaps even in prison. He seemed unable to think politically about rights and responsibilities, and appeared to focus more on his own family concerns. In contrast, Cherise, a child of a lone mother (and the same age), was more philosophical:

> I would say, Dad, if you're going to go away and leave me, you must go and do what you have to do to free your country. I'd be

sad [about the family splitting up]. I'd say why did you have to split up? In some ways you know you can't stay together, 'cos things ain't always forever. *Cherise*

Cherise's reaction suggests that she had considered the personal downside of Mandela's decision, but was able to subordinate this to a wider political agenda of rights and responsibilities.

Simon and Ibrahim asked me about Mandela's childhood. Learning that he came from the Transkei they asked how the situation in South Africa had come about.

Simon: If white people were there before the black people, then it should be the white people's.

Hilary: No, they came almost together, that's what interesting, to this bit of South Africa. So whose land is it?[7]

Ibrahim: They should share the land, just divide it in equal parts.

Simon: No that won't work, because if a black person accidentally just crosses the other person's land then it's machine guns and goodbye.

Ibrahim expresses a belief in sharing and equality of rights. Simon is sceptical. Moving from his view of 'finders keepers' he assumes that peaceful coexistence is impossible. It is possible that, as in his response about Winnie Mandela, he is not able to think outside the boundaries of personal experience. Earlier he had talked about the ongoing hostility between his family and neighbours forced to share a fence. He also revealed the extent of violence within his own family. Ibrahim was not without knowledge of land-related problems. His family had come from Bangladesh because of political difficulties there, and within the family there had been disputes about land they owned in Bangladesh. However, in contrast to Simon's jaundiced views about adults, Ibrahim told stories about a much admired father who went out of his way to help neighbours in trouble – suggesting experience of reason and tolerance in the home environment.

Given children's very different responses and experiences, with their implications for living harmoniously with diversity, teachers face a particular challenge. Moralising is clearly not a solution. Some knowledge about the children we teach is essential, for this provides insights about where they may be coming from. However, regardless of previous experience, the opportunity for children to discuss, explore issues, hear alternative viewpoints to their own, in contexts at one remove from their own lives, is an important first step towards understanding complex issues.

Risking your own life to help someone in danger of their life – the contrasting stories of friends and strangers: Miep Gies and Allen Jay

These two stories invite children not just to nail their colours to the mast with respect to racism and injustice, but also to follow through the limits of responsibility of ordinary people faced with morally indefensible situations. As with Mandela's story, it is quite easy to think of analogous contemporary situations in which we are not so much required to take personal action, but to take a view about interventions by the government of our country. All these children felt strongly and with no hesitation that it was right to come to the help of a friend, even at personal risk, possibly, because they were already familiar with Anne Frank's diary.

> 'Cos they're your friends, and you've known them for a long time. If I was actually there I wouldn't think at all, I'd just say yes. I wouldn't say no and I'll have to think about it, because the next day you go back and you find they're all dead and everything. *Simon*

Although all but Otto Frank later died in the camps, the children's judgement that Miep's decision to help was correct did not alter. But their justifications were different. For some, the principle was the main thing: you must do the right thing, regardless of the consequences with hindsight. If an action was right you had a responsibility to follow through. If you didn't, your conscience would not be clear. What made Miep's decision right, in their view, was her friendship and loyalty to the Frank family.

Hilary:	Was it worth it?
Emily/Harriet:	Definitely. If they could have lived, they would have had a better life, but if Miep hadn't helped them, they would have had a much shorter life.
Harriet:	You should always try to make things right, because it might work out all right, you never know, and if it sounds really stupid like trying to help them, and you know it won't work, at least you should try.
Ibrahim:	Yes, it was worth it, because you did your best you can to keep them alive. You did your best you can.

For others, the consequences for Jan and Miep justified the decision, suggesting that the children's judgement in hindsight would have been different, if those who helped the Frank family had been caught. Farzana put it simply: 'They (Jan and Miep) was right. They didn't get killed'.

In contrast, the children found the dilemma of helping the slave Henry James considerably more difficult. Although there was evidence of empathy and compassion for Henry's personal plight, particularly his wounded feet, and general condemnation of slavery, children were uncertain whether to put one's own family in danger for a stranger. The issue was also more complicated because they were being asked to think about a child helping an adult, rather than adults helping other adults and children:

> It's good if they run off because they can have freedom, if they don't run off, the slave's life is like a big wall in front of them ... but he [Allen] should try and make Henry understand what's going to happen. He should say, my house is going to get burned if they come, my whole family's going to be destroyed. He can't really help because he's going to go through so many risks, he can't just abandon his family. Allen can't do it all by himself. *Farzana*

> I really think Allen should help, because he believes that people shouldn't really be slaves. *Toyin*

> When Allen Jay was talking to the black man he was putting himself at risk, and he could be killed by his own people, and even

> though he was a Quaker and a Christian , and you're not supposed to... colour is not what matters, it's what's on the inside, he should have left it and said, I can't help you, because I would be putting my life at risk, if it's to help you. I can't do nothing, I don't want to be killed. *Cherise*

In contrast, Cherise had not hesitated that Miep should help the Franks, even though her life would be at risk. Yet Simon, who had wanted to stay out of the line of fire in the South African story said:

> I think he should take the risk. 'Cos like if his feet are bleeding he'll need help. ...Like if he helps this person then he's going to get hurt by other white people. But he's going to get in trouble, and his family, and he's thinking about his family, if they find out then his family will be killed, and he's thinking what should he do. It's a big risk to take. And he's in a dilemma. He should help him. *Simon*

Ibrahim, who typically considered other people's perspectives, added: 'He wouldn't like it if he was on the opposite side'.

Conclusions

This chapter has reported on the perspectives of eight children, drawing indirectly on the understandings of a total group of 22 students. Although it is impossible to generalise about the ways children will respond, it is clear that these young people, aged between 7 and 11 years, are developing individual personal stances to moral dilemmas. Some children are responding from an ethic of justice, rights and responsibility. Others make choices based on compassion or pacifism, taking care to establish details before coming to a conclusion. None starts from an empty ethical position, and each draws on their existing knowledge and experience. The research indicates that children are capable of far more than we normally credit or ask of them.

What is striking about all the children in the sample (and not just those who feature in this chapter) is their commitment to the dilemmas, and the care with which they engaged with the problems or expressed their attitudes. They all show a willingness to consider different perspectives, to reflect on the implications of decisions and to work to reconcile conflicting positions. Their ability to think hypothetically, to consider consequences of behaviour with a serious concern for morality and not just instrumentality, is impressive. The question remains of why we may be reluctant to do more of this kind of work in school. It is widely accepted that developing the capacities to think, act and decide in everyday contexts, where we are faced with intrapersonal and interpersonal dilemmas all the time, is part of education. Are we perhaps frightened to empower children and give them a voice which could lead to them questioning the morality of powerful people?

The national curriculum for England includes a values statement which claims to be a list of accepted moral positions which 'everyone' agrees upon, and which we should teach our children (QCA, 1999). Yet knowing the right or wrong thing to do in practical contexts is far from straightforward. To exercise both one's responsibilities and one's rights as a citizen requires sorting through conflicting demands and pressures to satisfy different agendas. The habits of mind required to carefully weigh up evidence and implications do not come instinctively; they need to be taught and practised. The implications for the citizenship curriculum are, I think, clear. Primary school is not too soon. It is fascinating to note that all the children, when asked, thought they were old enough to debate the issues in the stories – even the 7-year-olds.

Children may be more capable of thinking about the ethics of issues to do with racism, responsibility, intervention, and when it is right to challenge or even break the law than we give credit for. Unsurprisingly, some of their thinking will be governed by personal experience from which they may be generalising inappropriately. Some experiences may hinder them from thinking 'outside the box' and considering broader political and ethical terms. This is not a reason to avoid developing such political thinking. Teachers need to know their pupils, so that when, for example, someone like Simon reduces dealing with apartheid to dealing with his hostile neighbours, we can understand, but can also move him on.

We can use history to help appreciate wider issues. We can encourage children in a quest to look for causes beyond personal motivation, for a range of perspectives, for short and long term consequences, and to evaluate significance in the long term as well as the short. The teaching of history can have moral relevance, though not in the way that our Victorian ancestors wanted, to justify imperialism and the transmission of true British values all over the world. Instead, teaching and learning history can help children to consider the kind of world we live in and the kind of world we want, drawing on the experiences and moral challenges that people before us have faced, and the changes they have sought to bring about. History has a role to play in addressing the social and moral aspects of citizenship education.

References

Brill, M.T. (1993) *Allen Jay and the Underground Railroad*. Minneapolis: Carolrhoda Books.

Claire, H. (2001) *Not Aliens: primary school children and the PSHE/Citizenship Curriculum*. Stoke: Trentham.

Davenport, T.R.H. (1991) (4th edition) *South Africa: a modern history*. London: Macmillan.

Foley, A. (1973) *A Bolton Childhood*. Manchester: Manchester University, Extra Mural Department of the WEA.

Gies, M. and Gold, A.L. (1988) *Anne Frank Remembered: the story of the woman who helped to hide the Frank Family*. New York: Touchstone, Simon and Schuster.

Larrabee, M.J. (1993) Gender and moral development: a challenge for feminist theory, in: M.J. Larrabee (Ed.) *An Ethic of Care: feminist and interdisciplinary perspectives*. London and New York: Routledge.

Levstick, L. (2000) Articulating the silences: teachers' and adolescents' conceptions of historical significance, in: P. Stears, P. Seixas and S. Weinberg (Eds.) *Knowing, Teaching and Learning History*. New York: New York University Press with American Historical Association.

Noddings, N. (1986) *Caring: a feminine approach to ethics and moral education*. Berkeley: University of California Press.

Qualifications and Curriculum Authority (QCA) (1998) *Education for Citizenship and the Teaching of Democracy in Schools (The Crick Report)*. London: QCA.

Qualifications And Curriculum Authority (QCA) (1999) *The National Curriculum 2000*. London: QCA

Wolf, C. (1983) *A Model Childhood*. London: Virago Modern Classics.

Notes

1   Each child features in *Not Aliens*, where I use the same pseudonyms.

2   In the thirty years or so before the American Civil War ended slavery in the Southern States, a network of white and black people set up an escape route to the North. This clandestine route was nicknamed the Underground Railroad (see Brill, 1993).

3   Miep Gies features in Anne Frank's Diary. For Gies' own account of helping the Jewish families hidden in the attic in Prinsengracht, see Gies and Gold (1988).

4   Wolf's writing explores the 'official silences' about the pre-war era in Germany.

5   In 1960, only white people in South Africa had the vote. New laws had been brought in by the all-white South African Government, forcing black women as well as black men to carry passes wherever they went. There was widespread protest among the black population. The police opened fire on a meeting of unarmed people protesting at Sharpeville against the pass laws. 69 Africans were killed and 180 wounded. In the face of the people's anger, the Government declared a State of Emergency and became more repressive.

6   Ibrahim confuses slavery with apartheid, but his argument about standing up for your rights remains valid.

7   The 'Bantu' peoples of Southern Africa had been longstanding inhabitants of the interior and the East of Southern Africa when white people first arrived and settled, initially in the Western Cape. The indigenous people of the Western Cape were not Bantu but Koi and San. The first clashes between white and Bantu occurred in the Transkei/Ciskei areas of the Eastern Cape as the whites moved eastwards. Though the dates are disputed, it is generally thought that the movement south-west of Nguni people (the Mfecane) into the Transkei and Ciskei occurred not very long before white settlers started moving East, in the late eighteenth century (see Davenport 1991: 10-17).

8   Issues discussed here are explored in the travelling exhibition *Anne Frank + yoU*. See www.annefrank.org.uk

7

Citizenship education and students' identities: a school-based action research project

Anne Hudson

There is growing interest in the ways in which young people can participate in the development of their schools. Research suggests that young people's participation in decision-making processes may improve discipline (Osler, 2000) and may ultimately contribute to more effective learning (Rudduck and Flutter, 2004). Equally importantly, the UN Convention on the Rights of the Child confirms the participation rights of children and young people and, notably, their right to express their views in decisions that will affect them (Article 12). This chapter reports on the implementation of citizenship education within one school and the ways in which students were encouraged to acquire skills for community and school development. It will seek to demonstrate how this learning for citizenship and democracy in school had a significant impact upon students' perceptions of themselves, effects that contributed towards transforming relationships and approaches to learning. It will seek to show that while the implementation of citizenship practices are unlikely, in the short-term, to impact directly upon academic results, they may contribute towards the longer-term transformation of schools.

As Bernstein reminds us, participation is not only about discourse, about discussion and debate, it is also about practice, and a practice that must have *outcomes*. The right to participation 'is the right to participate in the construction, maintenance and transformation of order' (Bernstein, 2000: xxi). If a school is to develop as a community of practice for citizenship education, it must enable young people to participate in its transformation. Schools are complex institutions and seeking to change the school in this way can be an enormous risk. Those implementing change need to be clear about their aims and to be able not only to defend them but to persuade others to participate in the change processes. They require moral purpose:

> Moral purpose is one of change processes' strange attractors because the pursuit and pull of meaning can help organise complex phenomena as they unfold. (Fullan, 2000:18)

This chapter will illustrate how the processes of introducing citizenship education into the research school served as one such 'strange attractor' to give meaning and direction to the school community.

School context

In 1999 South Docks School in London began a campaign to become a specialist school for citizenship. Staff agreed to back this campaign partly because specialist status would bring additional resources to the school, but also because many believed a focus on citizenship was appropriate for a school developing strong relationships with community organisations and striving to promote awareness of civic society and civil duties. Although the government initially declined to recognise citizenship as a subject for specialist school status, the school was selected as a pilot for the introduction of citizenship education and received additional resources. Consequently, the school was able to appoint a youth and community worker as an additional member of staff to support the author in her role as citizenship coordinator, responsible for the development and implementation of this new area of the curriculum.

South Docks was, in many ways, a typical 11-18 inner-city comprehensive school with 1,216 pupils on roll, 56 per cent of whom were boys. The school population is ethnically and linguistically diverse, with 55 per cent speaking English as an additional language. The catchment area has a high rating on indexes of social and economic deprivation. The unemployment rate in the area was around 12 per cent and 49 per cent of students had an entitlement to free school meals (regarded as an index of poverty). 55 pupils were registered as having special educational needs (SEN), having various severe learning or behaviour difficulties. Student behaviour was often challenging. Standards of attainment were below the national average for England, but compared favourably with schools of similar intake.

Solidarity among the staff was strong. Teachers shared a deep commitment to social inclusion and to combating inequality. This ethos was an important factor in embracing the citizenship agenda. Two rather more unusual factors were the head teacher's willingness to take risks and a comparatively open style of management that appeared to enhance teachers' motivation and self-esteem.

Most South Docks students live locally, within walking distance or a short bus journey. Many students live on housing estates whose residents have experienced decades of relatively inconsequential regeneration expenditure. The area, as a leading local community organisation stated, 'remains deprived and its citizens disempowered' (New Cross Forum, 1999). Alongside a widespread and deeply rooted sense of powerlessness, there has been, over a 10-year period, a process of accelerating community mobilisation. This, too, made the school's commitment to citizenship pertinent.

Developing meanings for citizenship education
Teachers' changing understandings
At the start of the project, teachers were consulted about what form citizenship education could and should take in the school. The process included two residential weekends, each voluntarily attended by over 20 teachers. During this phase, citizenship was presented in terms of the areas of learning highlighted

by the government's advisory group on education for citizenship and the teaching of democracy in schools: knowledge and
understanding; skills of enquiry and communication; skills of
participation and responsible action (QCA, 1998).

Teachers generally endorsed the need for young people to learn
about the key concepts highlighted in the Crick report: democracy and autocracy; cooperation and conflict; equality and
diversity; fairness, justice and the rule of law; law and human
rights; freedom and order; the individual and community;
power and authority; and rights and responsibilities. During
2000, the school mapped citizenship opportunities and outcomes across the curriculum. It soon became apparent that it
would seldom be possible through this route to provide
students with specific citizenship learning experiences. Acquiring knowledge through active participation and working for
change would need a separate curriculum area. So from early
2000, teachers began to plan for a Citizenship Studies GCSE
course.

By 2003, at the end of the research cycle, some teachers noted
how the citizenship curriculum itself contributed to students'
understanding of topics within their subjects. They commented
on the pertinence of understanding democracy and being able
to distinguish between fact and opinion. Heads of departments
also reported that where there had been an active citizenship
dimension in schemes of work, notably in Geography and
Personal, Social and Health Education (PSHE), attainment was
higher and students were better motivated than usual. Other
teachers suggested that work in citizenship lessons had helped
developed students' speaking and listening skills.

Citizenship in the curriculum
From September 2001, all students in Years 10 and 11 (aged 14
to 16 years) had a weekly one-hour GCSE citizenship studies
lesson. Most units of work ended with some change-oriented
activity. For example, the unit on global politics and power
ended with students writing letters to the *Sun* and *Mirror* newspapers about their coverage of the war in Iraq. The students
were impressed to have replies to their letters and for their

views to be heard. At the end of the unit on globalisation, students chose either to make posters for the staffroom promoting ethical consumption and advertising fair-trade products or to write letters to the director of Nike about workers' conditions and pay.

In addition, assessed coursework promoted active citizenship and making a difference. Many students embraced the opportunities to investigate an issue that concerned them directly. They chose to engage in a variety of projects, for example, preventing mobile phone theft, improving local leisure facilities, dealing with bullying and making local streets safer. Students researched their areas of interest using surveys, photographs and video and presented recommendations to panels of local decision-makers. They evaluated their own work, and reflected on how they collaborated with other students.

Each class in Years 7 and 8 devoted a morning (equivalent to three one-hour lessons) to citizenship learning twice a term. The major focus during the first half of the year was an investigation of local leisure facilities, with students making recommendations as to how these might be improved. This was real situated learning: students undertook fieldwork in the local area, including photography and interviews, and developed presentations, which were delivered to people with power locally.

Interviews with a sample of 30 students across Key Stages 3 and 4 (Years 7-11) during the spring of 2003 included questions relating to the meaning of citizenship, one of which was: do you think learning about citizenship is useful? Student responses were almost entirely positive. There was a general tendency among students to identify citizenship learning with the specific issues they had investigated. So, for example, when commenting on the implications of their citizenship studies, they tended to assess the importance of the particular topic they had focused on, such as the community development issue they had investigated or the issue of fair trade.

Citizenship and school culture

In 1999 the school re-launched its School Council, providing relevant training for staff and students. By 2002, the Council was perceived by students as well as outside organisations as being effective and dynamic – a view supported by evidence collected in interviews for this case study. In 2002 a Students as Researchers project was launched to further enhance students' ability to influence school improvement.

Student identities

Interviews with students revealed that the project had an impact on their notion of the community to which they felt they belonged. Their replies reinforce citizenship as a feeling of belonging (Osler and Vincent, 2002) and demonstrate that citizenship learning is fundamentally linked to individuals' engagement and identities in the community. It is important to distinguish between 'personal identity', referring to the construction of the self, and 'social identity', which refers to the way that we locate ourselves within the society in which we live, according to such factors as class, gender and ethnicity (Bradley, 2003).

Identity and agency: a framework

Bradley (2003) identifies three levels of social identity: passive identities, active identities and politicised identities. He sees passive identities as potential identities in a sense that they

Figure 7.1: Relationship between agency and identity

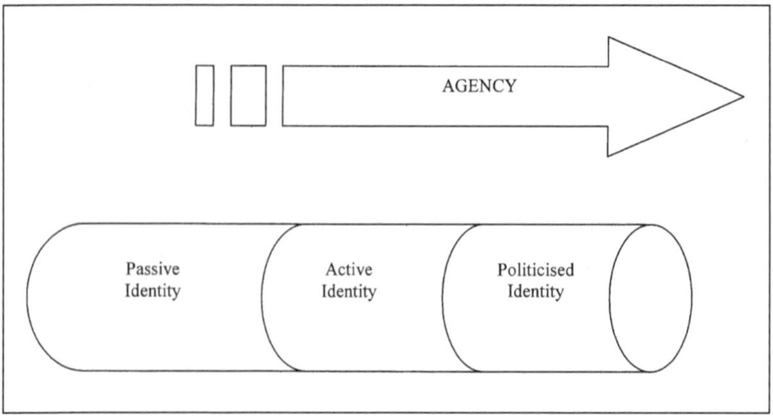

derive from the sets of lived relationships in which the individuals are engaged, but they are not acted on. Active identities are those that individuals are conscious of and which provide a base for their actions. Where identities provide a more constant base for action and where individuals constantly relate to these, they can be described as politicised identities. Figure 7.1 extends this analysis and applies it to learning and action in the community. If we see the three levels of identity as a continuum then they may be said to relate to an individual's growing sense of agency. As a person develops from a passive to a politicised identity, so that individual's sense of agency also develops. This is part of the process of citizenship learning. Agency – the notion of one's potential power over situations – grows as this learning and community engagement develops. Power is inescapably linked with control, both latent and manifest (John, 2003). Once young people sense and begin to exercise an internal locus of control (Wallace, 2000) their identities can become active.

Passive identity and shared belonging

For many students, who may not have had the inclination or opportunity to become active members of the school community, there was, nevertheless, an awareness that they were part of a shared school community enterprise. The project included two annual Citizenship Days. Surveys showed that the most popular aspect of these days, for students, was working with people in different year groups. The Citizenship Days undoubtedly promoted a sense of community. Participating in the citizenship mornings in Years 7 and 8 and the presentations of coursework by Year 10 and 11, students also served to promote the notion of belonging to a community of practice for citizenship. The term 'community' had become a new kind of artefact in the life of the school. It was used not only to denote the school itself as a community, but also to refer to the wider community of the locality and the school's catchment area.

Students' GCSE coursework topics emerged out of their community surveys in which members of the local community were asked what issues concerned them most. It appears that students' sense of belonging was reinforced by their discovery that issues of personal concern coincided with the concerns of the wider community and by their further investigation of these issues. Crime was the most frequently cited issue of concern within the community and 27 out of 128 students surveyed by the author chose crime as the focus of their coursework project; 15 chose to work on improving the school grounds and 15 investigated local leisure facilities.

In their written responses to the question as to whether everyone can 'make a difference' 74 out of the 136 students who responded mentioned the word 'community' in their answers. 25 students specifically referred to the need to 'work together' in order to make a difference. An overwhelming majority of students in Years 7 and 8, after a year's citizenship activities, used the word 'community' in their definitions of citizenship.

Active identity and student engagement
The GCSE Citizenship Studies coursework invited all students to engage in a 'change activity'. Many of these were publicly presented to people with power. In their written responses to the question about making a difference, five students explicitly used the word 'coursework', but another ten mentioned using evidence and 21 wrote about their presentations as examples of making a difference. They cited concrete examples, usually based on their own experience. More than one in four students made a link between doing coursework designed to affect the school or local community and seeing themselves as agents of change. Of 136 written responses analysed, only one was sceptical about whether school students can make a positive difference. Through participating in these learning and assessment activities, students were developing active identities.

The school programme appears to have encouraged students to consider partnership with agencies which they may previously have mistrusted. In writing about making a difference to the local community, 28 students wrote about the difference they could make to crime. The police were mentioned 30 times as partners in such change processes. This was interesting as, in discussions during lessons prior to the coursework activities, many students had indicated scepticism as to how trustworthy and reliable the police were. It would appear that the presence of police representatives at the presentation events and their responses to the students led them to revise their perceptions of the police. Given the sense of powerlessness expressed by members of the local community in relation to crime, it is significant that students' statements about tackling crime show such confidence.

Some students focused on the fact that people could pass information to the police:

> ...by telling the police who the thieves are because everybody knows who they are that are scared to tell the police. Have neighbourhood watches. More cameras in places people often get robbed, and tell the mobile phone company to make better security on the phones. *Layton, Year 11 boy*

Others stressed the importance of influencing people in positions of power:

> I think I can make a difference because I told my opinions to my group – we shared these with our year and an MP – and those people might then go on and do something about it or tell someone else, so making the Community more aware of such problems in society and then in the world. *Keeley, Year 11 girl*

> A few weeks ago we did make some kind of difference by presenting our research and findings about mobile phone theft to the local MP. The way we made this difference was by bringing up important issues which everyone knew about to present to people in power who can make that change which we desire ... many people agreeing means power and power means making changes. *Joshua, Year 11 boy*

The School Council was also seen as a direct means through which students could directly influence the school and the wider community:

> Everyone can make a difference by spending the form time discussing what is wrong and what needs to be done outside school. Some students can make a difference if they are part of the School Council it will get our points across to teachers who have the main power if our views go ahead. *Martin, Year 10 boy*

Many students gave concrete examples of the School Council's achievements:

> Pupils can make a difference now more than ever because of projects like these. We also have a School Council which put people's views through. Already in year 10 they have made a rule that you can wear hats in the playground, jumpers in playground and in the building, fixed up the toilets and organised some parties. So there are a lot of ways which pupils' views can easily be heard. *Mark, Year 11 boy*

These latter examples illustrate how receiving visitors and engaging in the School Council had given some students the experience of power, supporting the observation that: 'In order to learn about power, children need to be given opportunities to exercise it' (John, 2003: 48). The students' responses suggest they are developing active identities as citizens. Of course, this may be a temporary, situation-specific phenomenon (Solomon and Rogers, 2001). If this is the case then citizenship learning may need to support in further developing a sense of agency. Effective citizenship education might be said to be achieved when individuals develop politicised identities.

Politicised identities

If politicised identity is categorised as becoming operational where identities provide a more constant base for action and where individuals constantly think of themselves in terms of an identity, interviews with school council representatives suggest that many of their identities are 'politicised.' When asked why they chose to stand for the Council, several interviewees reported that they had done it before and considered it to be worthwhile:

> I believe the three years that I've been in the school council... I believe that we've improved more and we're getting more things that we want. Because in the School Council in Year 7 and 8 I don't think we got that much. But in these years we're really developing and getting a lot of things that we want. *Charlene, Year 10 girl*

> I have done it before and I thought it done quite well for the school and so I just wanted to be a part of that. *Emma, Year 9 girl*

Well the first year I tried, I didn't get through. I think that's because the pupils in class wanted someone with experience but when I actually started it I realised how it was helping me because I got more confidence in speaking out in public because mostly I would not do it. I would just sit down and watch someone else do it. It gave me other skills like running workshops and working with big presentations. It's quite amusing when you actually see yourself doing something like that because I didn't think I was going to do stuff like that. I wasn't expecting it because in our primary school we never had a school council so I didn't really know what it was about and I thought it would be a good experience to stand for School Council. So I did it last year and it was a really good experience and I thought I would do it again this year. *Mabina, Year 9 girl*

Asked how they felt about their work in the Council, all the respondents were very positive about their own efficacy:

It's helped the school so I'm quite pleased with that because it is what the School Council is about: to improve the school. *Emma, Year 9 girl*

I do think it's been effective because usually quite a lot of different points come up at each meeting and lots of them get sorted out, especially things to do with lessons and how teachers can improve themselves. *Theo, Year 9 boy*

Even more obviously 'politicised' are the identities of those students who chose to engage in the Council of Champions. Local community organisations in the catchment area of the school decided to set up a democratic forum to parallel the borough's official council. This organisation is called the Council of Champions. It was agreed that the Community Champions could be as young as 12 years old, and that anyone aged 12 or above could vote. Students at the school were encouraged to stand and vote for the Council of Champions and four were elected. Candidates had to write a statement for publication in a leaflet distributed to over 20,000 households locally for voting. Significantly, over half the Council of Champions are young people. The main goal of the Community Champions is to listen to local people, to stay informed about what's going on locally and to influence the organisations that make decisions that directly affect people's lives. Clearly, the decision to stand for election must be based on a fairly powerful sense of self-efficacy.

This was reinforced when the candidates were successful. For example:

> I chose to stand for the Council of Champions because I felt I could make a difference by putting my views and other people's views into action. Like issues to do with education and safety and housing issues ... I actually feel encouraged to do more things for the community. ... I've learned like how to go into the world to make a stand for myself. *Luke, Year 7 boy*

> ... I'm much sharper now. I feel more confident in myself and in my work. And that's really good. I can go to meetings now and actually talk. So School Council was really useful. (She was a school council rep in Year 7) *Anma, Year 8 girl*

Dynamic identity

For young people in particular, identity is fluid. As the arrow in Figure 7.1 shows, some students are in the process of moving from passive to active or active to politicised identity. The research showed that involvement in citizenship projects and activities was perceived by the students as enabling them to develop. In her often disturbing account of how young people survive abuse and develop, John (2003) relates development to challenge and risk. Success in confronting a challenge has a positive impact on young people's sense of agency.

The responses of students interviewed or those who provided written answers to the question about making a difference showed the importance of initial success in their sense of self-efficacy. Those who have gone on to stand a second time for the School Council, or who have moved from being Council representatives to standing for the Council of Champions; those who have successfully participated in projects such as Cash for Cans, the school grounds project or organising their Year parties and gone on to face other challenges are in the process of developing politicised identities. Being someone who believes she or he has the power to change things is such an identity.

Dynamic identity: developing the self

Students were asked, during the interviews, whether the citizenship project had changed them. Several respondents said they thought it had made them more 'mature':

> Yeah I think I'm becoming more mature ... seeing it from different points of view because now I can see it in the adult's perspective as well as my own. *Rita, Year 9 girl*

Others seemed to feel it had empowered them in other ways – for example enabled them to know where to go for information or support, or made them feel generally more capable:

> My friends say I do more things than I'm capable of. Like my friend said to me yesterday 'I'm quite shocked that you have really good grades and you still do all those things.' ...I have probably become more involved than I was before. *Anma, Year 8 girl*

One of the interview questions was designed to discover whether students' citizenship experiences had affected their identities in ways that extended beyond the school. Mabina certainly seemed to be aware of it:

> Yes. During the summer I went with Sadie to Wales and we had different activities which we had to do and we had to work with children we never met in our lives. We had to do some activities like we had to do rock climbing. We had to trust them to hold us up and stuff like that. It gave us a stronger trust between people you don't know like your first impressions of people can be quite strong. It has helped us relate to different things in our lives more. *Mabina, Year 9 girl*

Another example of promoting self esteem in this way came from Shadrack:

> Yeah. My friends sometimes say 'Look at your picture in the Oi magazine. I am a little famous star around my friends. It does because I have joined several clubs. So yeah it does affect outside of school. *Shadrack, Year 8 boy*

Dynamic identity: future self

Perhaps even more salient evidence could be found in responses to the question about how the work affects students' vision of their own future.. Rita was able to relate it to education:

> Yes because I believe that if we ... like in Students as Researchers if we do develop something that can build up on our education... Yeah, I'll have a better future. *Rita, Year 9 girl*

Other students reported that they felt their life choices had become wider:

> Yes. I might like... because I'm more confident I might like.. I don't know... be more like a speaking person. Like in conferences and stuff like that and like to organise stuff. Like be in a school and organise all the things. Like the rules and stuff like that. *Emma, Year 9 girl*

> Well, it helped me to be a bit more open minded about what I do in the future. Like I had one thing that I wanted to do but then the School Council made me look at what other options I could choose for a career. I wanted to be an actor but now I want to do something like helping with .. Maybe politics or something like that. *Theo, Year 9 boy*

Rights and responsibilities
A crisis of rights and responsibilities?

The ethos or culture of citizenship, particularly student voice, was to become an area of anxiety for teachers. Discussions with staff during the project's construction were structured in a way that separated the values, ethos and pedagogical issues from the knowledge and understanding. This attempt to simplify the citizenship project may have militated against a more desirable holistic approach to the concept. Locating it within the themes identified in the official government documents on citizenship education, it is now suggested, drew insufficient attention to political literacy and circumvented the notion of a human rights framework. A major thrust for developing the school's citizenship culture had been the development of student voice, particularly through the School Council. In the absence of directly confronting the potentially thorny issue of students' and staff's rights, there was little discourse addressing teachers' concerns and expectations about this.

Subsequent interviews with teachers revealed significant unease. Clearly, many teachers held notions of citizenship that emphasised students' responsibilities rather than their rights. There had been hopes, in several quarters, that the project would help improve student behaviour and generate greater respect for the school environment. The following excerpts from interviews with Heads of Year and Heads of Department testify to this:

I still think that they have difficulties with understanding the rights and the *responsibilities* part of it and my expectations were that they would become more involved in dealing with the responsibility side of it. *Head of Year B*

I think the difficulty's been the balance between rights and responsibilities. Because I do think from the point of view of the staff they see certain pupils that have been very very assertive but still don't have an understanding that there has to be a payback or there has to be some sort of balancing out. *Head of Department A*

The head teacher and some key staff recognised the difficulties arising from teachers' notion of the rights agenda. He actually referred to a 'crisis of rights and responsibilities,' commenting on the importance of understanding that the correlation between rights and responsibilities is part of a long learning process. Osler (2000: 55) writes about the 'misunderstanding of the nature of children's rights ' and 'fear amongst teachers that children's rights may be in opposition to the rights of teachers'. The research for this study certainly highlighted these misconceptions. It showed that in most cases the students were keen to embrace the responsibilities the citizenship agenda opened up for them. Indeed, the interviews with students indicated that some of them had begun for the first time to consider issues from the perspective of teachers and to recognise the importance of other points of view.

Rights and responsibilities: breakthrough and conflict

The research, which triangulated evidence from the view of students, staff and outsiders, revealed differences of perception. It suggested that the legacy of participation and reification (Wenger, 2001) in the initial construction of the project, particularly the absence of a human rights framework, brought limitations to the adults' senses of the meaning of citizenship. It showed that the adults viewed the impact of the project on the curriculum as significantly beneficial, to a greater degree than the students. Tensions were revealed between the students' sense of empowerment and being listened to and the adults' notion that the emphasis on young people's rights ignored implications for responsibility. Conversely, the adults appeared less aware than the students of its positive effects upon identity.

The development of identity as a sense of belonging to an effective community of practice was found to have a powerful positive effect upon students' attitudes towards the school and to have had a potentially beneficial effect upon relationships between students and staff.

Rights and responsibilities: changing relationships
Of the sample of students interviewed, nineteen responded directly to questions about the nature of relationships in the school. Nine of them responded with almost unqualified statements that relationships were good; five that teachers related well to students and two that pupils were generally respectful although teachers were not always. Only one student seemed to feel she had been treated unfairly, in this case by her peers rather than teachers. Students frequently articulated a growing ability to empathise with adults and teachers. For example:

> I have learned that actually pupils can work with teachers and be on the same level and get respect and get what we both want and we can communicate and discuss things that we all want together. Instead of teachers making all the plans we can actually tell them how we feel about things. So that's what I've learned. That we can actually discuss things. I think I have become more mature now. And I understand where teachers are coming from. *Chardelle, Year 10*

Sharing the research findings with the teachers would be an important next step of the change process. It underlines the reality expressed so succinctly by Fullan (2001:22) 'Conflict, if respected, is positively associated with creative breakthroughs...' It could raise awareness of the reality that, in addition to the noticeable impact on the curriculum, the young people in the school benefited in ways not immediately visible to teachers. Their positive identification with the community of practice for citizenship education had improved their perceptions of their relationships with teachers.

Schools as communities of practice for citizenship education: some lessons about inviting students into identities of participation

As Fullan (2001:22) notes, transforming the culture is the main point. Teachers' anxieties may diminish when the process of students identifying with the project and their community of practice is further advanced. Teachers will be able to discover how students' sense of being listened to enhances their commitment to the school community and its norms. Had this been evident at the point where some teachers became concerned about the balance of power, the process might have provoked less anxiety. For other schools embarking on such reculturing it will be helpful to visit schools where student voice could be shown to 'work'.

Sharing learning of this kind across schools could bring enormous benefits. Were the South Docks project to begin again, an important starting point would be to develop the whole community's understanding of human rights, including the relationship between rights and responsibilities. Clarity about the importance of active citizenship learning and political literacy would be high on the agenda too. School-based projects like this one are always context-specific, so that it could never be totally replicated. What the South Docks experience showed is that inviting students into identities of participation through citizenship education can begin to transform attitudes and relationships. South Docks' journey along that route thus far was possible largely because of its relatively democratic and open management style, a culture difficult to sustain in the era of the 'managerial school' (Gewirtz, 2002).

References
Bernstein, B. (2000) *Pedagogy, Symbolic Control and Identity.* Maryland: Rowman and Littlefield.

Bradley, H. (2003) *Fractured Identities: changing patterns of inequality.* Cambridge: Polity Press.

Fullan, M. (2000) *Change Forces.* London: Falmer Press.

Fullan, M. (2001) *Change Forces. The Sequel.* London: Falmer Press.

Gewirtz, S. (2002) *The Managerial School.* London: RoutledgeFalmer.

John, M. (2003) *Children's Rights and Power.* London: Jessica Kingsley.

New Cross Forum (1999) *Get Set for Citizenship: laying the foundations of neighbourhood renewal.* London: Magpie Resource Library.

Osler, A. (2000) Children's rights, responsibilities and understandings of school discipline. *Research Papers in Education*, 15 (1): 49 – 67.

Osler, A. and Vincent, K. (2002) *Citizenship and the Challenge of Global Education.* Stoke: Trentham.

Qualifications and Curriculum Authority (QCA) (1998) *Education for Citizenship and the Teaching of Democracy in Schools. Final report of the Advisory Group on Citizenship. 22 September. (The Crick Report).* London: QCA.

Rudduck, J. and Flutter, J. (2004) *How to Improve Your School: giving pupils a voice.* London: Continuum.

Solomon, Y. and Rogers. C. (2001) Motivational patterns in disaffected school students: insights from pupil referral clients. *British Educational Research Journal.* 37 (3): 331- 345.

Wallace, B. (2000) Able and talented learners from socio-economically disadvantaged communities, in: M.J. Stopper (Ed.) *Meeting the Social and Emotional Needs of Gifted and Talented Children.* London: David Fulton.

Wenger, E. (2001) *Communities of Practice: learning, meaning and identity.* Cambridge: Cambridge University Press.

8

Understanding the alien in our midst: using citizenship education to challenge popular discourses about refugees

Jill Rutter

Picture this scene. In a London suburban school, a young teacher of citizenship is preparing to teach a Year 9 class (13 to 14-year-olds). From the scheme of work, he notes that there is a twelve-week unit devoted to human rights. One lesson focuses on asylum-seekers and refugees as examples of people who have lost their rights. The teacher invites students to formulate their own definitions of refugees and asylum-seekers. Some of the more vocal students write: 'asylum-seekers are money-grabbing terrorists'. Later, the teacher reflects on what happened. He admits the lesson did nothing to challenge popular prejudices about refugees and asylum-seekers. Instead, it provided a platform for crude stereotypes drawn from the tabloid press. This was a real scenario observed by the author. Well-meaning citizenship teachers in many schools teach similar lessons. Not only are these lessons ineffectual in promoting an understanding of human rights, at worst they may reinforce stereotypes and the present scapegoating of refugees and asylum-seekers.[1]

This chapter considers how citizenship education might promote diversity and challenge racism. In particular, it considers
how the citizenship curriculum might empower students to
critically examine popular discourses about refugees. It
examines the link between these discourses and policy developments, comparing attitudes to refugees at the beginning of the
twenty-first century with those expressed one hundred years or
so earlier. The chapter reports on research, conducted between
1999 and 2001, which examined how children in English schools
see refugees in their midst. Drawing on this research, it suggests
strategies which teachers and schools might adopt to challenge
racism more effectively.

Historical constructions of refugees

At the end of the nineteenth century, Jews fleeing oppression in
the Russian Empire, Romania and Austrian Galicia started
arriving in the UK. From 1886, Jewish immigration emerged as
a problem in popular discourse, with Arnold White, an anti-
immigration author and campaigner, presenting the Jewish
migrant as the 'pauper foreigner' (*The Times* 13 July, 1887).
Workers in London, including dockers and shoemakers concerned about being undercut by this new group, agitated for
restrictions on immigration (Fishman, 1975: 76). They were
joined by some right-wing Conservative politicians. One MP,
Major-General Evans Gordon, went on to form the antisemitic
and anti-immigration British Brothers League. The anti-
immigration stance of these workers and politicians was reflected in the populist press, including the *Daily Mail*. Many
members of the Anglo-Jewish community, anxious to protect
the image of their own community, expressed concerns about
the numbers of immigrants and were fearful that the existence
of a new visible Jewish community would arouse antisemitism
(Fishman, 1988: 149-155).

The discourses used by anti-asylum activists in the late nineteenth and early twentieth century share a number of features
with the anti-asylum discourses prevalent at the beginning of
the twenty-first century. The newcomers, referred to as aliens,
were seen as:

- ▓ a cause of unemployment and overcrowded housing

- ▓ dependent on public funds, for example 'The so-called refugees', *Daily Mail*, 3 February 1900)

- ▓ dirty and diseased (House of Commons, 1888: minutes 1367-1730)

- ▓ dangerous political radicals

- ▓ a vast under-enumerated mass

- ▓ undercutting English wage labour (House of Commons, 1888 minutes 2483-2662).

From 1900, immigration restriction was included as part of the Conservative Party's policy. Eventually, the Aliens Act 1905 was passed, marking the first modern immigration legislation.

Public opinion was not hostile to all refugees. The 250,000 Belgian refugees who arrived during the First World War, following the German invasion of Belgium, received a warmer welcome, and were portrayed as brave heroes, 'the plucky little Belgian' of the popular press (Kushner and Knox, 1999: 52). There was little resentment expressed, except in London where there were anti-Belgian riots in 1916. Indeed, at the peak of public support, concerned citizens established over 2,500 local Belgian refugee committees. This level of public support for refugees has not been matched since (Holmes, 1988; Myers, 2001).

Then, as now, public discourses about refugees were ambivalent, complex and fluid. They are often also localised. Yet there are many similarities between discourses today and those aired a century ago. Then, as now, the media played a major role in constructing public views about refugees.

Refugee policy: closing the door

From the late 1960s, British immigration policy began to restrict primary immigration, passing legislation such as the Commonwealth Immigrants Act 1968 and the Immigration Act 1971. During most of this period, asylum was not a political issue: it was largely divorced from debates about immigration, race and racism. This changed in 1989. This year saw worsening human rights in Sri Lanka, the Democratic Republic of Congo and eastern Turkey and a worsening civil war in Somalia. The period 1989-1993 saw a major increase in UK asylum applications, primarily of Sri Lankan Tamils, Congolese, Turkish Kurds and Somalis. Asylum became a political issue, with asylum-seekers seen as another group of primary immigrants and measures put in place to restrict their entry.

The British Government has developed a four-pronged approach in changing asylum policy:

■ barriers that prevent asylum-seekers arriving in the UK

■ deterrent measures that make settlement in the UK more difficult

■ tightening the criteria by which the Home Office judges an asylum application

■ a democratic deficit in immigration and asylum practices, with greater emphasis on immigration rules and on secretive attempts at the European harmonisation of asylum practices (see www.statewatch.org.uk).

Since 1987 there have been six Acts of Parliament targeted at asylum-seekers (see Table 8.1). Arguably, it is 'deterrent measures', mainly restrictions of rights to benefits, work and housing, that have had the greatest effect on race relations. The Asylum and Immigration (Appeals) Act 1993 denied asylum-seekers the right to permanent social housing. Homeless persons' units in local authorities were required to check an individual's immigration status before providing housing, a measure driven both by immigration control and the need to cut public spending (Morris, 1998). As this legislation passed through Parliament, the tabloid press began to label asylum-seekers as scroungers and benefit fraudsters.

The Asylum and Immigration Act 1996 restricted access to benefits, allowing only those who applied for asylum at the port of entry to claim income support. Those appealing against a negative decision also lost access to benefits. Instead, asylum-seekers became the responsibility of local authority social services departments. Families with children were supported under the provisions of the Children Act 1989 and given a cash allowance and some form of temporary accommodation. Those without children were supported under the provisions of the National Assistance Act 1948 (in Scotland, the Children Act [Scotland] 1995 and the Social Work [Scotland] Act 1968).

What resulted was a chaotic system detrimental to both asylum-seekers and local government. Asylum-seekers were left cashless and unable to purchase bus fares, books, clothing,

---

Table 8.1: UK asylum legislation and policy changes 1987-2004

1987 Immigration (Carriers' Liability) Act fines airlines and shipping companies for transporting passengers who do not have the correct documentation.

1987 Social security regulations change, restricting asylum-seekers' allowances to 90 per cent of income support.

1989 Visas introduced for Turkish nationals after Kurdish asylum-seekers start arriving in the UK, as a deliberate attempt to block entry. Since then visa requirements have been introduced after the arrival of significant numbers of asylum-seekers from particular countries.

1993 Asylum and Immigration (Appeals) Act restricts access to social housing for asylum-seekers. Introduces fingerprinting.

1996 Asylum and Immigration Act stops welfare benefits for in-country asylum applicants. Further restricts their access to social housing. Employers obliged to check the immigration status of employees.

1999 Immigration and Asylum Act sets up the National Asylum Support Service (NASS), a Home Office department that provides vouchers for asylum-seekers and housing in new areas of dispersal.

2001 Ending of the voucher system of support, after a campaign led by refugee organisations, faith groups and trade unions.

2002 Publication of *Secure Borders, Safe Haven: integration with diversity* White Paper on immigration and asylum.

2002 Nationality, Immigration and Asylum Act
Removal of right to work from asylum-seekers

2004 Asylum and Immigration (Treatment of Claimants) Bill before Parliament. Allows for electronic tagging of adult asylum-seekers.

second hand goods and even the cheapest forms of entertainment, such as a cup of coffee. By 1997, there was a shortage of hostel type accommodation in Greater London. London local authorities began to move asylum-seekers out of the capital, often to seaside towns. Cashless, unsupported and with nothing to do, these asylum-seekers were a visible group who attracted more adverse media coverage. Local authorities were not fully compensated by central government for the services they provided for destitute asylum-seekers. The latter grew increasingly unpopular with some officers and councillors. Political leaflets produced for local elections detailed the cost to local people of having to support asylum-seekers. Some of the less scrupulous councils briefed the press. Headlines such as 'Influx of refugees costing thousands' (*Kettering Evening Telegraph*, 7 August 1998) and 'Old Folk's Home to be hostel for refugees' (*Harrow Leader*, 16 July 1998) became commonplace. Popular discourses focused around costs to local people and the notion of asylum-seekers being unworthy of support.

Due to growing public hostility and concerted lobbying from local authorities, the Government was forced to take back responsibility for them. Rather than restore benefits, the Immigration and Asylum Act 1999 introduced a new support system for asylum-seekers administered by the National Asylum Support Service (NASS), part of the Immigration and Nationality Department of the Home Office. Once asylum-seekers have lodged their application, they can apply to NASS for support. NASS offers two options: support and accommodation or a 'support only' package. Support means a cash allowance, amounting to about 70 per cent of income support. People with nowhere to stay are usually dispersed out of London, to NASS-commissioned housing in different parts of the UK. Since dispersal of asylum-seekers was introduced, there has been a huge increase in racial attacks on asylum-seekers, documented by the Refugee Council and other organisations (Refugee Council, *Inexile Magazine*). Dispersal was accompanied by negative media coverage and pronouncements from politicians likely to cause concern. Asylum-seekers have been murdered in Glasgow and Sunderland.

It has been argued that the dispersal scheme has effectively dispersed racism and anti-asylum sentiments, previously focused on London and the South East (Fekete, 2001). Government failure to make sufficient healthcare and educational provision may have also increased public hostility. The Government may also have increased anti-asylum sentiments by focusing on the need to cut asylum numbers – Tony Blair's commitment to halve asylum numbers by October 2003 (Home Office, 2002a). Good race relations, it is argued, depends on keeping down refugee numbers. In focusing on numbers, the Government constructs an image of hordes of people seeking to enter to UK.

The Nationality, Immigration and Asylum Act 2002 made provision for accommodation centres for some asylum-seekers. Planning applications for accommodation centres have been a focal point for anti-asylum campaigns (ICAR, 2004). At the time of writing, the Home Office is planning further changes to the asylum support scheme. Instead of moving to NASS accommodation, some asylum-seekers may, in future, be required to reside in these centres, each housing about 800 people. Here, asylum-seekers will receive full board, healthcare and education. Despite being very expensive to build and maintain, the Home Office is clear in its justification of the new accommodation centres. They are meant to prevent asylum-seekers working illegally (Home Office, 2002b). More importantly, accommodation centres are intended to ease the removal of failed asylum applicants – by preventing them from putting down roots in local communities.

Discourses on asylum seekers have changed. The asylum-seeker has again emerged as a threat to public health: 'HIV Soars by 20%, migrants blamed for increase' (*Sun*, 25 November, 2003). Following a number of similar headlines, the Government put the Asylum and Immigration (Treatment of Claimants) Bill before Parliament in 2004. Among its clauses are those that remove the right to non-emergency healthcare to asylum-seekers whose applications have failed.

Since 11 September 2001, and increased concerns about security, the asylum-seeker is also portrayed as a potential terrorist. Equally disturbing is a new anti-asylum discourse: that asylum means mass immigration and greater cultural diversity. Such diversity is presented as a threat to 'British values' and is said to threaten community cohesion. It has been argued that support for the welfare state is dependent on citizens feeling they are supporting those who are like themselves (Goodhart, 2004). This debate has been aired by broadsheet newspapers, as well as tabloids (see, for example, *The Guardian*, 24 February 2004).

Impact on communities: a case study

The scapegoating of asylum-seekers has undoubtedly contributed to increased racism, including violent attacks on refugees. Refugees from Iran, Turkey, Somalia, Sudan and Sri Lanka have been murdered in the UK. For every murder there are hundreds of thousands of incidents of racist abuse and racist attacks, most of which go unreported. The majority of perpetrators of racial harassment are young.

Racial violence is perpetrated by a small number of individuals, but for this to happen, there is almost always tolerance of racism within the larger community, as well as widespread negative feelings towards ethnic minority groups. The case study presented in Box 8.1 indicates how such negative perceptions can develop and how they can ultimately lead to violent attacks. It also suggests that, if efforts are made to work with and consult local people, such hostility can be diffused.

Events similar to those described in Box 8.1 have taken place across the UK. The case study shows that factors contributing towards the racial harassment of refugees may include:

■ existing local tensions

■ high unemployment and poor housing

■ negative portrayals of refugees in the local media, particularly concerns about crime

■ inflammatory statements by local politicians

■ ill-planned dispersal of asylum-seekers

▨ no local consultation over plans to house asylum-seekers

▨ little previous settlement by ethnic minority communities

▨ failure by the police to pick up on growing tensions and to protect victims effectively

▨ failure of schools to challenge hostility to refugees from non-refugee students and their families.

Box 8.1: Case study of impact of the asylum-seeker dispersal policy

X is a small industrial local authority in northern England. From 1999 London local authorities began to house asylum-seeking families and single people there. The same year the authority also received Kosovans arriving as part of the Kosovan Humanitarian Evacuation Programme. Later, the local authority agreed to receive asylum-seekers dispersed by NASS.

The local authority planned to commission housing for some 180 NASS-supported asylum-seekers in a hostel in a former pit village. The hostel was to be built and run by a private company. There was no consultation about the hostel, but news of it leaked to local people, who were very angry. As a result there were considerable local objections. On one occasion, police were called to a meeting about the hostel because the council official who was there to hear concerns feared for the safety of himself and his colleagues.

The proposed hostel site was close to sheltered housing for the elderly. Some of the sheltered housing residents organised a sleep-out protest on the site of the planned hostel. The protest attracted substantial coverage in the local media, with refugees described in very negative terms. Some press coverage described refugees as beggars or members of armed gangs.

The protests were followed by racial attacks on refugees already living in the area. At least three refugee children were attacked on their way to school. At the same time at least sixteen asylum-seeking children were refused school places, with headteachers conceding to the pressure of local parents.

In Summer 2000 Refugee Council staff working in the town held a community-based meeting to talk to organisations working in the area, as well as to concerned local residents. They explained why asylum-seekers were being moved to the local authority and sought to dispel myths. The meeting was successful in that many local residents and members of tenants' associations were brought on the side of refugees. The climate in the local authority has improved since this initiative, although the planned hostel was not built (Rutter, 2003).

Everyday school experiences of refugee students

Refugee students' experiences of racism in schools mirror what is happening in the wider community. Studies on the experiences of refugee pupils reveal that many experience racial harassment in their schools and neighbourhood. In one study in the London Borough of Hackney, 32 refugee children were interviewed. They were from a range of national groups, including Bosnians, Turkish Kurds, Somalis and Vietnamese. All the children were judged by their parents and teachers to be coping in school but nineteen of them reported that they had suffered racial harassment and nine had moved school as a result (Richman, 1995).

Peer-led research among refugee children in London (Save the Children, 1997) found that over half of those interviewed reported bullying in their schools and over 25 per cent reported the existence of racism, although fewer freely admitted to personal experiences of bullying (15 per cent) or racism (30 per cent) (Save the Children, 1997). The children in the research were targets of racism from both white and black UK-born students. Most commonly they were referred to as scroungers. Some children reported that they were taunted by calls of 'asylum-seeker' and 'bogus'. Less than half the refugee children knew if their schools had anti-bullying or antiracist policies and these were rarely seen as effective. Research carried out with asylum-seeking children settled in Glasgow, found that their greatest concerns were about racism and safety (Save the Children, 2002). These studies confirm the findings of the author's own research, in which over half of children interviewed reported racist bullying, most usually verbal taunts, which usually related to themes aired in tabloid newspapers (Rutter, 2004b).

What can schools do to challenge racism?

Under the Race Relations (Amendment) Act 2000 schools are required to promote race equality and to prevent discrimination; one of the practical implications is that they have a race equality policy. In order to promote good practice, schools need to engage in four key areas of work:

■ evaluate previous antiracist work

■ promote multi-agency working: how does the school work with other agencies to challenge racism, including parents, the police, youth groups, tenants' organisations, Race Equality Councils, football clubs, local authority housing departments

■ ensure effective monitoring and sanctions against who perpetrate racist bullying

■ use the school curriculum and extra-curricular activities to promote diversity and equality. The citizenship programme of study for secondary schools in England (QCA, 1999) includes the obligation to teach about 'the diversity of national, regional, religious and ethnic identities in the United Kingdom and the need for mutual respect and understanding'. (Klein, 1993; CRE, 2000)

Citizenship education has been advanced as a way of addressing racism. Yet as we can see from the opening scenario in this chapter, there are many pitfalls.

How can citizenship education make a difference?
Examining popular discourses
The Refugee Council has produced a book, *Refugees: we left because we had to,* (Rutter, 2004a) which aimed to find out how young people viewed asylum-seekers and refugees and to evaluate what might comprise good practice in challenging racism. Targeted at young people aged 11-18 years, it includes background information, refugee testimonies and student activities. It draws on the existing literature and on my own ethnographic research in schools and provides ideas which might be used in classrooms to challenge racism directed at refugees and to support students in thinking critically about popular discourses.

Challenging racism
Research in Greenwich offers important insights into challenging racism. Hewitt (1996) observed that antiracist and multicultural education policies had had an impact on changing the attitudes and behaviour of many school pupils but noted that

there remains a core of racist youth in the predominately white areas he studied. He observed that although Greenwich has a diverse population, it is divided, with certain areas where ethnic minority communities do not live or even visit. This divide was perpetuated in housing policy. From his work with white youth he concluded:

■ the peer group was the main agent in the reproduction of racist attitudes and that this group also played a greater role in policing of racist attitudes than did parents

■ most children in predominantly white areas had little social contact with children from ethnic minority backgrounds until they entered secondary school, by which time they were becoming aware of themselves as part of a specific peer group

■ the majority community played down the racist element of violence and abuse

■ local authority antiracist policies were widely interpreted by the majority community as being 'unfair to whites', stoked by coverage of antiracist initiatives in the right-wing tabloid press

■ two domains of school activity were considered 'unfair to whites': discipline and the ways in which cultural differences were addressed

■ some schools dealt with disciplinary incidents in a way that stressed the school's antiracist policy rather than asserting the fundamental wrong of the offence

■ schools often portrayed minority cultures as unitary, in events such as 'Africa Week'. (Hewitt, 1996)

The research stresses the need to portray cultures in true-to-life complex forms. Simplified portrayals may exclude majority students and prevent them from identifying with the culture in question, leading them to feel they have no culture of their own. Antiracist initiatives in schools need to run side by side with practices that address other oppressions, such as poverty and sexism.

Developing empathy

The Refugee Council has also carried out research with young adults in an attempt to identify strategies that could be adopted by refugee agencies to generate sympathy towards refugees (Rainey *et al.*, 1997). The researchers interviewed two groups of young adults, none of whom had strong views on immigration or refugees. The interviews highlighted that refugees in the UK are not seen as part of everyday life, as they are 'hidden away' in hostels. As none of the interviewees had had any social contact with refugees, it was easy for media stereotypes to take hold. Although many interviewees expressed superficial sympathy towards refugees, this was not coupled with identification. Refugees' backgrounds and plights were considered to be 'other-worldly'. The use of statistics and hard facts had limited use in challenging popular stereotypes of refugees. Rather, education programmes need to stress that refugees are ordinary people in extraordinary circumstances. One strategy is to draw on personal testimony and ask 'how would you feel if ...?' questions. As one interviewee explained: 'Instead of making it a charitable thing – oh look at the poor refugees – it makes you think about refugees as people like you'.

Understanding through social contact

Ethnographic research in six different locations in the UK, where asylum-seekers had been dispersed or might be housed at a future date, highlighted worries about asylum-seekers in these communities. Many of the concerns, misconceptions and stereotyping of asylum-seekers and refugees were fluid and sometimes localised, but fear of crime and concerns about stretched public resources were common to all areas. National media coverage was often provocative in stoking these concerns (ICAR, 2004). The researchers suggest that social contact with asylum-seekers and refugees is important in lessening misconceptions and concerns. Their report also stresses the importance of host communities being given accurate information about asylum-seekers, but notes that information alone may not always be effective in dampening concerns and challenging racism.

Developing the citizenship curriculum

In order to identify how the curriculum might better support an understanding of refugees and asylum seekers, I conducted research in four schools, two in London and two in South East England. My analysis also draws on field notes made on visits to schools during the 1990s, while working as education adviser at the Refugee Council. My aim was to find out how students in the school viewed asylum-seekers and refugees and how the school had used citizenship education to raise awareness about refugees. Citizenship education was defined in its broadest sense to include cross-curricular and extra-curricular events. In each school, I interviewed key teachers and presented questionnaires to each class. Some students were also interviewed. All four schools taught about asylum and migration. Two of the schools were located in or near areas where the British National Party had stood candidates in local government elections. There were refugees in all the schools, although numbers varied: they comprised 20 per cent of the school population in one school, but less than fifteen students in another.

The research confirmed that children's views about asylum-seekers and refugees were rather fluid and often localised. In the early 1990s, few children knew who asylum-seekers were – the term refugee was used to describe those who had fled from their own country. By 1997, the term asylum-seeker was being used by school students, almost always in a pejorative way. Refugees were constructed as people they had to help, often objects of pity. Asylum-seekers, however, were constructed as 'bogus' or 'scroungers'. One child, when asked the difference between an asylum-seeker and a refugee stated: 'We have to help refugees, but asylum-seekers have come to get free housing'.

During the early 1990s, children talked about refugees taking jobs and housing. By 2000, discourses about asylum-seekers focused on the cost to the public purse of supporting them, and on fears of crime. During 2002, fears emerged of asylum-seekers being potential terrorists. Children's views about asylum-seekers and refugees often reproduced what had been featured in the tabloid media. For example, one school visit was made in the days following a series of articles about asylum-seekers having a high incidence of HIV. Student discourses reflected this, for example: 'Refugees need medical help' and 'Yes, helping refugees, that's where all our money goes. Refugees have got AIDS, that's where all our money goes, for them'.

There were very few moral discourses about refugees in any school visited. Students did not appear to consider or debate moral issues such as whether it is right to allow housing and benefits to asylum-seekers, or to deny anti-retroviral treatment to asylum-seekers who have failed to secure asylum in the UK (a practice that has become health policy since April 2004).

In the two schools situated outside London, children viewed asylum-seekers as being responsible for crime, housing shortages and overcrowding – what they felt was wrong about London. Field notes made in northern England also confirm this notion of London as being synonymous with migration, overcrowding and crime.

On a more positive note, some students in all four schools voiced support for asylum-seekers and refugees and stated concerns about them being stereotyped by the tabloid media. Students in the two London schools articulated most support, suggesting that social contact with refugees might have changed attitudes. However, there was a real mismatch between attitudes articulated by students and student behaviour. In both the schools, teachers and students reported that young refugees were subject to verbal abuse and racist bullying. Most refugee pupils did appear to be rather isolated in all schools, excluded to a significant degree from wider friendship groups.

Interviews with students and teachers attempted to evaluate some of the curricular and extra-curricular initiatives in each of the four schools to make students more aware of asylum-seekers. All these had been planned by teachers who were concerned about how refugees were portrayed in the media and treated in the environs of the school. They comprised:

∎ Two citizenship lessons, taught as part of a unit on human rights, supplemented by some teaching in the history and geography curriculum. Students listened to video testimony of refugees.

∎ A six week unit on diversity in the UK, of which one lesson was about refugees, supplemented by a visiting speaker from a refugee organisation.

∎ A short programme of work in citizenship and English on 'journeys', with input from an actor and writer who was himself a refugee. Students also viewed video of personal testimonies of refugees.

∎ A curriculum unit on race and diversity, with other inputs from geography, history and English. The latter focused on the portrayal of refugees in the media. In this school, planning across departments was strong and there was a strong welcoming ethos. The school also ran high profile Refugee Week events that involved contributions from all students.

Conclusions and recommendations

The research pointed to some important issues for citizenship educators working to challenge the racism experienced by so many refugees. Schools that had a welcoming ethos appear to be the most successful in challenging racism and promoting diversity. Schools that involved all parents in work about diversity in equality were also more successful in challenging racism.

The allocation of time resources appears to be a key factor that determines if a curricular initiative about refugees is successful or not. Time needs to be allocated to teaching about issues such as diversity, racism and migration. A one-hour input about refugees will not change pupils' conceptions and misconceptions, or their behaviour towards refugees in their school and neighbourhood.

Another key factor in determining the success of citizenship initiatives in lessening the hostility expressed to asylum-seekers appears to be the potential of young people in being able to *do* something to support refugees, rather than passively absorb information about refugees. In three of the schools – children asked questions about how they could help refugees, often expressing frustrations about not knowing what to do. These supportive children were willing to engage as active citizens, to support refugees in their school and local community.

The most effective teaching began with the personal experiences of refugees, through the use of refugee speakers or video testimonies. This approach mirrors that used in much Holocaust Education – people first, then the event (Imperial War Museum, 2002). In this way students see refugees as human beings, rather than statistics or the dehumanised victims of war and persecution.

Educational approaches that stress our common humanity, challenge negative stereotypes and the construction of refugees as 'alien other' appear to be the most effective in challenging hostility to refugees. Approaches that stress past British experiences of forced migration, such as child evacuation during the Second World War, also appear to be effective.

Global citizenship appeared to be an intangible concept in all four schools. Students did not see themselves as global citizens or understand the notion of interdependence. Instead, they saw national self-interest as being most important, and unconnected with global politics. Teachers were not always confident in addressing national and local discourses about asylum-seekers and refugees or local issues relating to race, migration and asylum. Since these issues are fundamental to citizenship education in contexts of diversity, teachers require initial and on-going training and support in addressing these issues with students.

Arts education (creative writing, poetry, testimony and the visual arts) appears to be particularly successful in promoting diversity and challenging racism. The geography curriculum, however, with its emphasis on population inflows and outflows and the impact of migration, if taught without reference to wider social issues, may reinforce prejudice. However, arts education alone is not enough, as citizenship education is about politics. Young people need to be empowered to be involved in political decisions – at a school, local, national or international level.

Non-refugee school students need to be given the opportunity to debate controversial issues such as the reception of refugees in the UK. They need to feel that their opinions are heard. But some skill and sensitivity is needed in handling such debates, so as not to give a platform for racism. Students need to be given the opportunity to consider moral issues.

The curriculum cannot be seen in isolation from behaviour. Poor pupil behaviour in citizenship lessons undermines attempts to examine perceptions of refugees. Social contact with refugee pupils in schools is not effective, on its own, in challenging misconceptions and hostility. Schools are most effective in including refugee students when they plan opportunities for children to work together on joint projects and form friendships.

Schools and citizenship educators cannot challenge racism in isolation from the rest of society. They are most effective when they work with other service providers and organisations. Many local authorities have multi-agency working groups on race equality. Citizenship educators need to think about the ethos of their schools and give sufficient time to teaching about refugees, perhaps by working in partnership with other subject areas. Finally, students need to be empowered to take action to support refugees, locally, nationally and globally.

Recommendations

1. Within schools, curricular initiatives to challenge racism and promote diversity and equality must be coupled with other practices such as effective sanctions against pupils who perpetrate racial harassment.

2. A minimum of fifteen hours of work is needed in order to change pupil attitudes and behaviour.

3. Schools need to develop opportunities for students to engage in active citizenship to support refugees.

4. Schools need to use first-hand, personal testimonies of refugees, ideally by inviting refugee speakers who are prepared to talk to students.

5. Schools need to stress our common humanity and make links between refugee experiences and those of students and their families.

6. Students (and teachers) need further support in understanding the concept of global citizenship, including rights and responsibilities (see Osler and Starkey, 2000; Osler and Vincent, 2002).

7. Teachers need to be aware of national and local discourses about asylum-seekers and refugees and of local issues relating to race, migration and asylum and given training and support in addressing these issues in the curriculum. Citizenship education initiatives need to be able to respond to these national and local concerns.

8. Arts education, combined with citizenship education that stresses political literacy and the empowering of students, should be part of efforts to challenge prejudice and promote understanding of refugees and their situations.

9. Students need to be given the opportunity to consider and debate moral issues.

10. Schools need to involve all parents in work about diversity and equality.

11. Schools need to provide structured opportunities for non-refugee and refugee students to work together on joint projects.

12. Schools need to work with other local agencies to challenge racism and promote diversity and equality.

References

Commission for Racial Equality (CRE) (2000) *Learning for All: standards for racial equality in schools*. London: CRE.

Fekete, L. (2001) *The Dispersal of Xenophobia*. London: Institute of Race Relations.

Fishman, W. (1975) *East End Jewish Radicals*. London: Duckworth.

Fishman, W. (1988) *East End 1888*. London: Duckworth.

Goodhart, D. (2004) Too much diversity? *Prospect*, February.

Hewitt, R. (1996) *Routes of Racism: the social basis of racist action*. Stoke: Trentham.

Holmes, C. (1988) *John Bull's Island: immigration and British society 1871-1971*. London: Macmillan.

Home Office (2002a) *Press Release*, October.

Home Office (2002b) *Secure Borders, Safe Haven: integration with diversity. White Paper*. London: Stationery Office.

House of Commons (1888) *Report of the Select Committee on Emigration and Immigration [Foreigners]*. Hansard.

Imperial War Museum (2002) *Reflections*. London: Imperial War Museum.

Information Centre on Asylum and Refugees (ICAR) (2004) *Understanding the Stranger*. London: ICAR.

Klein, G. (1993) *Education Towards Race Equality*. London: Cassell.

Kushner, T. and Knox. K. (1999) *Refugees in an Age of Genocide*. London: Frank Cass.

Morris, L. (1998) Governing at a distance: the elaboration of immigration controls in the British economy, *International Migration Review*, 32(4): 949-973.

Myers, K. (2001) The hidden history of refugee schooling in Britain: the case of the Belgians 1914-18, *History of Education*, 30(2): 153-162.

Osler, A. and Starkey, H. (2000) Human rights, responsibilities and school self-evaluation in: A.Osler (Ed.) *Citizenship and Democracy in Schools: diversity, identity, equality*. Stoke: Trentham.

Osler, A. and Vincent, K. (2002) *Citizenship and the Challenge of Global Education*. Stoke: Trentham.

Qualifications and Curriculum Authority (QCA) (1999) *Citizenship: the National Curriculum for England*. London: QCA.

Rainey Kerry Campbell and Roafe (1997) Refugees: from a small issue to an important cause. Unpublished report. London: Refugee Council.

Refugee Council *Inexile Magazine*. On line at: www.refugeecouncil.org.uk/publications/index.htm.

Richman (1995) They Don't Recognise our Dignity: a study of young refugees in the London Borough of Hackney. Unpublished report. City and Hackney Community NHS Trust.

Rutter, J. (2003) *Supporting Refugee Children in 21st Century Britain*. Stoke: Trentham.

Rutter, J. (2004a, third edition) *Refugees: we left because we had to*. London: Refugee Council.

Rutter, J. (2004b) *Sold Short: education policy and refugee children*. Buckingham: Open University Press.

Save the Children (1997) *Let's Spell It Out: peer research by the Horn of Africa Youth Scheme*. London: Save the Children.

Save the Children Scotland and Glasgow City Council (2002) *Starting Again*. Glasgow: Save the Children Scotland.

Note

1   The terms 'asylum-seeker' and 'refugee' both have a specific legal meaning. An asylum-seeker is someone who has crossed an international border in search of safety, and refugee status, in another country. In the UK asylum-seekers are those awaiting a Home Office decision that would allow them to remain. To be granted refugee status a person must have left his or her own country or be unable to return to it 'owing to a well-founded fear of being persecuted for reasons of race, religion, nationality, membership of a particular social group or political opinion' (Article 1, UN Convention Relating to the Status of Refugees, 1951).

9

Teaching for equality and diversity: putting values into practice

Chris Wilkins

A changing agenda?

It is not enough to rely on the positive inclination of teachers towards an equality and diversity agenda. Teachers need effective support and this implies that both initial teacher training and continuing professional development programmes explicitly and significantly address questions of equality and diversity. This chapter explores teachers' attitudes towards teaching in a multicultural society and their perceptions of their roles in educating young citizens for the 21st century.

The role of schools in addressing social justice, and particularly their role in addressing race equality, has long been the subject of fierce debate among educationalists, politicians and policy-makers. From the 1970s, when systematic evidence of the underachievement of Black children in the UK school system emerged, the advocates of assimilation, multiculturalism and antiracism have argued their case and taken their message to the classroom (see, for example; Stone, 1981). This contentious culture, perhaps inevitably, led most schools, fearful of charges and counter-charges of indoctrination from left and right, to adopt a cautious, minimalist approach to race equality in the curriculum.

In the 1990s, two key developments changed the balance of the debate concerning the role of schools in fostering social values. First, the racist murder of black teenager Stephen Lawrence in 1993 and the subsequent inquiry into the investigation of his murder, instigated by the newly-elected Labour administration in 1997. The report of the Stephen Lawrence inquiry found that institutionalised racism permeated our society (Macpherson, 1999) and was widely seen as a wake-up call for a society that had thought that racism was a dwindling legacy of less enlightened times. In response, the government passed the Race Relations (Amendment) Act (RRAA) 2000, imposing an obligation on all public bodies (including schools and local education authorities) to actively promote race equality. Secondly, the murder in 1995 of London headteacher Philip Lawrence led to a public outcry about violent street culture in UK cities and the alienation of many young people from civic society. The government set up an advisory group on citizenship and democracy in schools, chaired by Bernard Crick, to address these concerns about violence and alienation among the young. Following the publication of the Crick report (QCA, 1998), citizenship education was introduced into the national curriculum in England in 2000.

This chapter draws on research tracking a group of teachers through their initial teacher training into the early years of their teaching careers, and exploring their attitudes to the role of schools in shaping social values. It draws on interviews, conducted in the mid-1990s, with students training to be teachers, which explored their role in developing citizenship education. A small sample of these beginning teachers were again interviewed in 2003 and were invited to discuss the potential of schools to develop an awareness of issues of diversity and equality. The study included an examination of the teachers' attitudes towards race equality issues, including their understandings of the changing nature of racism in society and the role that education has to play in challenging racism. It sought to set their concerns within a broad educational and social policy framework.

The 1990s have been characterised as a period of perpetual revolution, involving increasing prescription in many aspects of schools' work. The shift in the social agenda for schools brought about by the introduction of citizenship education into the curriculum and the requirements of the RRAA to promote racial equality reflects a tension between the narrow standards-driven agenda of education policy and a socially-transformative one.

Race in the classroom

In the late 1970s and early 1980s, mounting evidence emerged highlighting not only the failure of the education system to meet the academic and social needs of ethnic minority children, but its lack of attention to educating *all* children about the changing and diverse culture of the UK (Stone, 1981). There was a gradual change of emphasis in attitudes towards ethnic minorities from one of *assimilation*, the expectation that immigrants should adopt the lifestyle of the indigenous population, to one of *integration*, where cultural pluralism would prevail in an atmosphere of mutual respect and understanding. The Swann Report (DES, 1985) was highly influential in promoting the idea of multicultural education as the most effective approach to developing racial harmony.

Since the 1980s, classroom practice in multicultural education has generally been based on the study of 'other' cultures through an anthropological examination of their external features, frequently through the medium of religion (Parekh, 1986). This approach has been criticised for its narrow 'microscopic' view of race and culture, rather than a 'periscopic' anti-racist perspective which views culture in an institutional and structural social context (Mullard, 1985). The merits and limitations of multicultural education have been exhaustively debated (see, for instance, Modood, 1992; Carrington and Short, 1996; Cole, 1998). However, whilst this political and academic debate has continued, classroom practice relating to issues of ethnicity and culture has been dominated by a multi-culturalist perspective. Most significantly, this approach to addressing race equality was reinforced by the Crick report, which provided the underpinning philosophy for curriculum guidance on citizenship education (see Osler, this volume, chapter 1). This marks a missed opportunity for developing a more radical, challenging approach to race equality in the classroom.

From the mid-1980s and during the 1990s, schools were restricted in the impact they could make in addressing equality issues by a prevailing political climate that viewed education for equality as being incompatible with the pursuit of standards and excellence. The Conservative administration elected in 1979 made educational reform a high priority and attacked a profession seen to be dominated by a dangerous left-wing agenda of social indoctrination. The introduction of a national curriculum in 1988 was, in part, an attempt to reduce the freedom of teachers to select both teaching style and content and to promote a 'back to basics' agenda dominated by a focus on core skills and knowledge. This marked a shift from the broadly progressive, egalitarian approach of the 1970s and the traditionalist agenda of the 1980s.

During this period, the debate over the role of education was a confrontational one, with successive governments hostile to an educational establishment portrayed as egalitarian and socially-transformative. The assault on egalitarianism in education, which began with the Black Papers in the 1970s and was continued throughout the 1980s by groups such as the Hillgate Group (see, for example, Scruton, 1986) had a profound and lasting impact on education policy. This 'discourse of derision' (Ball, 1990: 32-42) inevitably left schools wary of tackling issues likely to be deemed controversial. In one notable example, legislation was actually introduced with the intention of preventing discussion of social issues in schools. Section 28, a clause of the Local Government and Housing Act 1989, meant that a generation of teachers felt unable to address issues of sexuality in the classroom.

The back to basics agenda survived the election of the Labour government in 1997. David Blunkett, the first Secretary of State for Education in the new administration, although an advocate of citizenship education and the minister responsible for this curriculum innovation, made no secret of his distaste for any other concern in education outside the narrow context of the raising of academic standards. It is not surprising, therefore, that in this climate, the demands made on schools as a result of the Crick report on citizenship education (QCA, 1998) and the Stephen Lawrence inquiry report addressing racism (Macpherson, 1999) seem to contradict the broader thrust of educational policy. For many teachers, the more immediate demands of raising standards, as measured by nationally standardised testing and a rigorous external inspection regime, have continued to dominate practice over the desire to address broader social goals.

Citizenship education and race equality

The advisory group on education for citizenship and the teaching of democracy in schools was established in response to a perceived democratic deficit and apparent disengagement of young people from civic and political activity. Concern over falling political participation of young people was raised almost to a level of 'moral panic' in press coverage (Osler 2000b: 26) and is supported to a degree by the findings of numerous studies of social attitudes over the past decade (see Wilkinson and Mulgan, 1995; Crewe, 1996; Jowell *et al.*, 1996). However, whilst there is evidence across a wide age range of disengagement from mainstream political activity (voting, political party membership) the focus on the particular alienation of young people is contradicted by evidence that suggests that, where the definition of political activity is widened to take account of volunteering and campaigning, young people's participation has, in fact, increased over recent decades (Roker *et al.*, 1999).

The introduction of citizenship education as a statutory element of the national curriculum, enacted in the curriculum review of 2000 (QCA 1999), should have been an opportunity for raising the profile of race equality issues across the curriculum.

The Stephen Lawrence inquiry report, published in February 1999, as the Qualifications and Curriculum Authority was drawing up the new curriculum guidelines, recommended that education play a major role in combating racism (Macpherson, 1999). The government responded by declaring citizenship education as the main vehicle through which this might happen in schools. The RRAA, with its requirement for schools to actively promote racial equality, was a direct result of Macpherson's findings.

Despite this shift in wider political discourse about race equality, the Crick Report is conspicuous in its avoidance of direct reference to racism. In this, it is consistent with the trend of the deracialisation of educational policy, subsuming 'race' amidst a range of other social categories and reducing racism to the level of individual ignorance and prejudice (Gillborn, 1995). As a result, whilst racism clearly remains a significant problem in UK society, and the RRAA demands that schools address institutional racism, there is little explicit encouragement within the curriculum for schools to challenge racist attitudes. The issues raised by Macpherson are to an extent sidestepped (Skinner and MacCullum, 2000).

The Crick Report does make reference to the need for promoting tolerance and diversity, with an emphasis on combating personal prejudice, and aims:

> to find or restore a sense of common citizenship, a national identity secure enough to find a place for the plurality of nations, culture, ethnic identities and religions long found in the United Kingdom. (QCA, 1998: 17).

However, for Crick, 'common citizenship' appears to require a degree of cultural homogeneity, and in emphasising the problematic nature of cultural diversity, the report as a whole underplays the structural nature of racism that is a significant factor in the political alienation of many young black people. (Osler, 2000b).

One of the most problematic aspects of the Crick report is its reliance on questionable assumptions setting out different citizenship priorities for different ethnic groups: whilst the majority 'must respect, understand and tolerate minorities', minorities 'must learn and respect the laws, codes and conventions as much as the majority' (QCA, 1998: 17-18). These statements not only distinguish 'minority cultures' by their difference from a presumed majority (white English) but also problematise them. The assumption is that there is a particular need to inculcate mainstream social values and that a pressing citizenship requirement is for minorities to learn the ways of the majority culture. In making assimilation a requirement, the report reflects not only a failure to understand the concept of racism, but fails to adopt a genuine human rights perspective, recognising that citizenship rights are claimed on the basis of true equality (Osler and Starkey, 2000: 14-15).

The danger of this conceptualisation of the 'multicultural' society is illustrated by the anti-Islamic response in the UK in the wake of the 11 September 2001 terrorist attacks on the USA. Representatives of the Muslim community were continually exhorted to condemn the attacks not only by the popular media but by senior government ministers (Richardson, 2004). The subtext of this approach is that members of minority communities, in this case Muslims, should be assumed to hold allegiance elsewhere unless they explicitly declare otherwise. Throughout the Crick report, common citizenship and pluralism are set in opposition to each other. Difference is emphasised over commonality and this difference is 'inextricably linked to conflict and dissent' (Osler, 2000b: 29).

Overall, the Crick Report is rooted in a depoliticised multiculturalist perspective that locates racism in the personal domain, a phenomenon of individual ignorance and prejudice, and suggests that through teaching about other cultures, the white majority will come to understand (and so respect and tolerate) minorities. Multicultural education is sited in a liberal social ideology of equality of opportunity, emphasising 'the enhancement of individual life-chances not on the diminution of group inequalities' (Jeffcoate, 1984: 186). Within this conceptualisation, the classroom is essentially a neutral arena in which tolerance can be fostered by understanding, and equality of opportunity can be achieved through the personal enlighten-ment that ensues.

However, RRAA takes schools a step beyond this minimalist agenda, placing on them a duty to promote race equality. This implies a proactive approach to challenging racism, including the institutional racism identified and acknowledged within the Stephen Lawrence inquiry report. There remains the question of whether the curriculum guidelines for citizenship education, themselves a diluted model of that proposed by Crick, provide an adequate platform for developing an antiracist curriculum.

Research process and methodology

The research process included a questionnaire survey of 418 students undertaking one-year full-time Postgraduate Certi-ficate in Education (PGCE) courses (both primary and secon-dary) at two of the largest teacher education institutions in England. The questionnaire sought information about stu-dents' political affiliations and actions, and explored their attitudes to a wide range of issues, including welfare and wealth redistribution; class, 'race' and gender issues; and environ-mentalism. From this it was possible to build comprehensive portraits of students' world-views.

Following the questionnaire survey, a sample group of 26 stu-dents, identified as being on the liberal-progressive-tolerant end of various social attitude scales, were interviewed at key points during their training year. The aim was to explore how their broader social attitudes and their own citizen identity impacted on their notions of their social role as a teacher and the role of schooling as a socially transformative process. In particular, the role of citizenship education was explored. More detailed accounts of methodology can be found elsewhere (Wilkins, 1999, 2001 and 2003).

Since the original research, two sets of follow-up telephone interviews have taken place with the original sample (now a reduced group as individuals have moved on, left teaching or contact has been lost), the first taking place in autumn/spring 2001/2002. The second set of interviews took place during the latter half of 2003, with the sample reduced to ten teachers (six primary and four secondary). In 2003 the opportunity was used to explore with the group, several of whom are now in senior management positions (with one of the primary teachers an acting head teacher), views on how schools can put the race equality mission of the RRAA into practice.

Student attitudes to race equality

The original research with postgraduate trainees produced some contradictory results with respect to racism in UK society. In interviews the students tended to locate racism in the personal domain and made little reference to institutional, structural racism. The questionnaire data suggested that respondents believed that racism was a persisting feature of UK society, and one that was embedded in institutional state practice (Wilkins, 1999: 222). While the majority stated that racism was a significant problem in society, there was a strong perception that this was largely due to individual fear and prejudice. Students suggested that the changing nature of British society, with its increasing cultural diversity, would lead to a steady reduction in racist attitudes:

> It's just ignorance really, lack of exposure to other cultural influences. If you only hear about people second-hand, you tend to end up with stereotypes, with a really exaggerated, one-sided view... I went to school in South London, so always spent a lot of time with other cultures... I think I have a reasonable insight ... I don't think a lot of white people have any idea what it's like to be black in this country. *Primary student, 1996*

> I think younger people are different, mainly because they've been brought up in multiracial communities, they've had black friends and been to school with them since they can remember, you know? We don't have the same hang ups. *Secondary student, 1996*

Students' belief that 'prejudice reduction' can be achieved through 'multicultural exposure' is problematic (see, for example, Mullard, 1985). If racism is to be effectively challenged in schools, it requires teachers who are prepared to challenge the social structures that create and reinforce the personal prejudice through which racism manifests itself. Almost all of the students felt that schools had an important role to play in fostering positive attitudes towards race equality, but lacked a clear vision of how they as teachers could act as agents of social change.

Teacher responses to race equality

As they progressed in their teaching careers, the tension expressed between a desire to challenge injustice and finding effective ways to achieve this has not gone away. In fact it appears even more noticeable. All of the teachers interviewed in 2003 gave the impression that it had become more difficult to incorporate a social dimension to their teaching, although the desire to do this had generally increased. Overwhelmingly, the reason cited for this difficulty was the pressure of working within a highly prescriptive curriculum model backed up by an inspection regime perceived to be punitive and narrow in scope. For one teacher, the opportunity to think about the bigger picture provided by this interview process was all too rare:

> I can't even think of the last time I thought about this stuff, not properly...it comes on daily basis, the way you interact with children...but I don't know that it comes into planning. Planning is about following the strategies...[the National Literacy and Numeracy Strategies] *Primary teacher, 2003*

Both primary and secondary teachers felt their ability to be flexible and creative increased with growing classroom experience but that they were working in a system that meant narrow, short-term, subject-driven objectives dominated their teaching. Above all, the external inspection framework (carried out by the schools inspection agency Ofsted) was blamed by teachers for the frustrations they experienced in meeting their pupils' and society's needs:

> It still doesn't matter...[what motivates you]...at the end of the day you've got to play the Ofsted game. They want to see the ticks in boxes and that means you play safe. No school's going to take risks... I think doing antiracist work, anything that's challenging, controversial...it's sticking your head above the parapet, and no-one wants to do that. *Primary teacher, 2003*

This safety-first mentality could be found in each of the teachers' accounts. One primary deputy head teacher was, however, more positive about their ability to deliver a broader social message:

> I think we try pretty hard really... at [the school] we have policies in place... I think we're pretty committed to tackling... [race equality]... head-on. This comes from the head, really... she's Asian and I think it makes a difference... it gives a message. *Primary teacher, 2003*

For this teacher, who was a member of the school's management team, equality issues were given a high priority. She was also aware of strong support from the local education authority. For those teachers who were not part of the management structure, the potential for change seemed less clear:

> I find it frustrating, I'd like to deal with some of the problems we have ...racism is a big problem here, and the school knows about it, but, it doesn't go much beyond dealing with it as a bullying issue, and that's a management problem. It goes deeper than that, we should be tackling the root problem, which is where most of our kids are coming from...we should be using [the curriculum] much more to challenge their ideas. *Secondary teacher, 2003*

Discussion

The teachers' views need to be seen in the wider context of the social and political culture of Britain, as most of them came to adulthood in a changing social climate, where the collectivism of the post-war era was discredited by the Conservative right and the rhetoric of individualism – freedom, choice and opportunity – dominated. We might therefore expect this generation, in particular, to be especially conscious of tensions between this individualist culture and the expectation that teachers should adopt an explicit social agenda, one which fosters civic virtues of responsible, active citizenship, and actively promotes racial harmony.

When interviewed as students, most were convinced by the argument that prejudice can be reduced through cultural exposure. They tended to assume that prolonged exposure to a range of cultural influences, through living in a diverse environment, was sufficient to promote harmony and understanding. Yet, this is to ignore the links between discriminatory attitudes and structural inequalities. Rather than challenge stereotypes, cultural exposure can reinforce them, and it appears to have little impact on underlying values (Gaine, 1995).

However, by 2003, and after six years' teaching, this previously widely-held viewpoint appears to have shifted significantly for many. The teachers perceived their efforts at changing attitudes and values had had very little impact. Their previous confidence in a 'permeation' model of cultural pluralism and tolerance had waned. There also appeared to be a growing frustration, particularly among the primary teachers, that they expended much time and energy in dealing with cultural issues in the classroom, but without feeling particularly well equipped to do so. During training, the students reported that dealing with equality and diversity issues was one of the most challenging aspects of their work (Wilkins, 1999). Six years later, over half the teachers interviewed felt the same way.

The initial research phase identified a small but significant number of negative and sometimes hostile responses to race equality issues (Wilkins, 2001). Perhaps unsurprisingly, these views were more openly expressed through anonymous questionnaires than through face-to-face interviews, although several *were* prepared to discuss their attitudes openly. By 2003, however, the participants in this research had been whittled down to a group who had from the start been situated on the liberal-progressive-tolerant end of the various social attitude scales produced, and so it has not been possible to follow up those individuals with less positive attitudes. However, those interviewed reported experiences which suggest that many teachers lack awareness of institutional racism. Almost all the teachers reported examples of attitudes and behaviours amongst colleagues that amount to a staff-room culture which is resistant to change. This reflects, perhaps, pragmatic concern with the immediate demands of responding to a somewhat narrow, utilitarian curriculum rather than outright hostility to the principles of equality in education.

Where next? Citizenship, equality and teacher education
This study charts the progress through training and the early years of teaching of a group of individuals whose social attitudes and values, their worldview, are fundamentally predisposed towards a society based on mutual respect and tolerance. All, to a greater or lesser degree, are committed to seeing education as a socially transformative process, and take seriously their role as social educators. Their commitment is, however, offset by pessimism about the impact they are able to make on the attitudes and values of their pupils. In particular, they tend to believe that structural constraints arising from a narrow policy focus on standards and basic skills hinder equality initiatives. Whilst they are aware of the need to promote racial equality, many teachers fail to engage fully with the social processes that create and reinforce racism. If teachers' concepts of racism remain rooted in the personal domain, then they will find it difficult to address the structural inequalities in education, including the attainment gap which exists between pupils from different ethnic groups. Effective teaching requires that teachers engage in a critical reflective process, and this in turn requires a depth of understanding not only of learning and teaching processes, but of the social context in which they take place.

The implications for initial teacher training and the continuing professional development of teachers are profound. Over the past decade or so, there has been a strong governmental steer to shift the emphasis from *education* to *training*, from a model based on praxis, the synthesis of theory and practice, to a narrow functionalist model of professional induction. The teachers taking part in this research felt constrained by the rigours of their training, and it was perhaps inevitable that the constraints were not appreciably lifted as they have entered an increasingly demanding professional environment. Despite this, many remain committed to the pursuit of egalitarianism and social justice through education even though they believe the curriculum and testing regimes are in tension with their goals. These findings are consistent with other research (Gillborn, 1995).

The utilitarian political climate of teacher training is in marked contrast with the renewed focus on wider social issues in schools, generated to a large degree by the introduction of citizenship education. Although the antiracist agenda appears to have been sidelined within the field of citizenship education, the requirements of the RRAA demand a more proactive approach from schools and local education authorities, and this has recently been recognised by the Department for Education and Skills (DfES). The consultation paper *Aiming High* (DfES, 2003), designed to support efforts to raise achievement of minority ethnic pupils, was set firmly in the context of the RRAA, and stressed the duty of schools to develop an ethos where racism is challenged.

Aiming High places race equality in education at a higher level on the government's education agenda than it has ever been. It signals recognition of previous failures in tackling under-achievement and a commitment to a positive approach to combating racism, acknowledging the negative impact racism has had on both educational attainment and on 'social cohesion'. The *Aiming High* initiative is less clear about the role of the curriculum in realising this commitment. Citizenship education, for example, receives only cursory attention. If the laudable aims of *Aiming High* are to be translated into action, senior management in schools and local education authorities will need to provide the support and encouragement for teachers to implement change in classrooms.

Equally importantly, teachers will require support in their initial training to develop a critically reflective approach to social justice issues with a clear antiracist dimension in their classroom practice. It is essential that the teacher-training curriculum acknowledges the critically transformative potential of education, the role of the teacher as a 'transformative intellectual' (Hill, 1989: 21-22).

A cause of concern amongst teacher trainers is that the Teacher Training Agency (TTA), the government body that regulates provision, has failed to fully acknowledge the race equality agenda in schools. Although the climate of training remains largely functionalist, the revised national requirements for initial teacher training give a much higher profile to racial equality and equal opportunities (TTA, 2002). Despite the difficulties of developing programmes designed to raise 'critical consciousness' in new teachers within the current framework, there is some evidence of a cultural shift.

The introduction of citizenship into the national curriculum, despite the minimising of the relationship between citizenship education and antiracist education, provides a clear opportunity for educators to address both issues in a coherent way. This opportunity is timely, given the new DfES interest in challenging racism through education. It is important, however, that the teacher education community develops closer links with schools and local education authorities to develop programmes of ongoing support for teachers (both initial and continuing) that keep citizenship education and race equality at the heart of the pupil experience. It is also vital that government agencies, both those concerned with curriculum development and delivery, and those concerned with the inspection of learning and teaching, maintain their current commitment towards increasing the status of these aspects of school life. Effective citizenship education must be underpinned by a framework of human rights and an understanding of structural inequality (Osler, 2000a), and this requires that teachers see themselves as agents of social change. If this opportunity is grasped, citizenship education can be employed as a catalyst for promoting equality, enabling children also to see themselves as genuine social agents who will shape society.

References

Ball, S.J. (1990) *Politics and Policy Making in Education: explorations in policy sociology.* London: Routledge.

Carrington, B. and Short, G. (1996) Antiracist education, multiculturalism and the new racism, *Educational Review,* 48: 65-77.

Cole, M. (1998) Racism, reconstructed multiculturalism and antiracist education, *Cambridge Journal of Education,* 28: 37-48.

Crewe, I. (1996) *Political Communications: the general election campaign of 1992.* Cambridge: Cambridge University Press.

Department of Education and Science (1985) *Education for All: final report of the Committee of Inquiry into the education of children from minority groups* (The Swann Report). London: HMSO.

Department for Education and Skills (DfES) (2003) *Aiming High: raising the achievement of minority ethnic pupils.* London: DfES.

Gaine, C. (1995) *Still No Problem Here.* Stoke: Trentham.

Gillborn, D. (1995) *Racism and Antiracism in Real Schools.* Buckingham: Open University Press.

Hill, D. (1989) *Charge of the Right Brigade: the radical right's attack on teacher education.* Brighton: Institute of Education Policy Studies.

Jeffcoate, R. (1984) *Education and Cultural Pluralism.* Lewes: Falmer.

Jowell, R., Curtice, J., Park, A., Brook, L. and Thompson, K. (Eds.) (1996) *British Social Attitudes: the 13th Report.* Aldershot: Gower

Local Government and Housing Act 1989 London: HMSO.

Macpherson, W. (1999) *The Stephen Lawrence Inquiry.* London: Stationery Office.

Modood, T. (1992) On not being white in Britain: discrimination, diversity and commonality, in: M. Leicester and M. Taylor (Eds.) *Ethics, Ethnicity and Education.* London: Kogan Page

Mullard, C. (1985) *Race, Power and Resistance.* London: Routledge and Kogan Paul.

Osler, A. (Ed.) (2000a) *Citizenship and Democracy in Schools: diversity, identity, equality.* Stoke: Trentham.

Osler, A. (2000b) The Crick Report: difference, equality and racial justice, *Curriculum Journal,* 11(1): 25-37

Osler, A and Starkey, H. (2000) Citizenship, human rights and cultural diversity, in: A. Osler (Ed.) *Citizenship and Democracy in Schools: diversity, identity, equality.* Stoke: Trentham.

Parekh, B. (1986) The concept of multicultural education, in: S. Modgil, 1986 (Ed.) *Multicultural Education: the interminable debate.* London: Falmer.

Qualifications and Curriculum Authority (1998) *Education for Citizenship and the Teaching of Democracy in Schools (The Crick Report).* London: QCA.

Qualifications and Curriculum Authority (1999) *The Review of the National Curriculum in England, the Secretary of State's Proposals.* London: QCA.

Richardson, R. (Ed.) (2004) *Islamophobia: issues, challenges and action. A report by the Commission on British Muslims and Islamophobia.* Stoke: Trentham.

Roker, D. Player, K. and Coleman, J. (1999) Young people's voluntary and campaigning activities as sources of political education, *Oxford Review of Education,* 25: 185-198.

Scruton, R. (1986) The myth of cultural relativism, in: F. Palmer (Ed.) *Antiracism – an assault on education and values.* London: Sherwood Press.

Skinner, G. and MacCullum, A. (2000) Values education, citizenship and the challenge of cultural diversity, in: R. Bailey (Ed.) *Teaching Values and Citizenship across the Curriculum: educating children for the world.* London: Kogan Page.

Stone, M. (1981) *The Education of the Black Child in Britain: the myth of multiracial education* London: Fontana.

Teacher Training Agency (TTA) (2002) *Qualifying to Teach: handbook of guidance.* London: TTA.

Wilkins, C. (1999) Making 'good citizens': the social and political attitudes of PGCE students, *Oxford Review of Education,* 25: 217-230.

Wilkins, C. (2001) Student teachers and attitudes towards race: the role of citizenship education in addressing racism through the curriculum, Westminster *Studies in Education,* 24 (1): 7-22.

Wilkins, C. (2003) Teachers and young citizens: teachers talk about their role as social educators, *Westminster Studies in Education,* 26 (1): 63-76.

Wilkinson, H. and Mulgan, G. (1995) *Freedom's Children: work, relationships and politics for 18- to 34-year-olds Britain today.* London: Demos.

Contributors

James A. Banks is Russell F. Stark University Professor and Director of the Center for Multicultural Education at the University of Washington, Seattle. His books include *Teaching Strategies for Ethnic Studies, Educating Citizens in a Multicultural Society*, the *Handbook of Research on Multicultural Education*, and *Diversity and Citizenship Education: Global Perspectives*. Professor Banks is a past president of the National Council for the Social Studies (NCSS) and of the American Educational Research Association (AERA). He is member of the Board on Children, Youth, and Families of the National Research Council and the Institute of Medicine of the National Academy of Sciences. He is also a member of the National Academy of Education.

Hilary Claire is senior lecturer at London Metropolitan University where she teaches history and educational studies. She was brought up under apartheid in South Africa – which has left an indelible mark – and came to England as an adult, working for many years as a primary school teacher. Her books include *Reclaiming Our Pasts: equality and diversity in the primary history curriculum*; *Not Aliens: primary school children and the PSHE/Citizenship curriculum*; *Gender and Education 3-19* and *Teaching Citizenship in Primary Schools*. In 2001 she co-founded the Primary Educators Network for the Advancement of Citizenship (PENAC).

Carole Hahn is Professor of Educational Studies at Emory University in Atlanta, USA, where she teaches courses in social studies education and comparative education. She was the US national research co-ordinator for the IEA Civic Education study. Her book *Becoming Political: a comparative perspective on citizenship education* and monograph *Educating a Changing Population: challenges for schools* examine issues of citizenship education in five multicultural democracies. She has also written articles on human rights and civic education in the United States. Carole Hahn is a past president of the National Council for Social Studies (NCSS), the professional association of social studies educators in the US. Her article 'Gender and civic learning' won NCSS' exemplary research award.

Anne Hudson is deputy principal in a south London comprehensive school and a part-time PhD student at the Centre for Citizenship and Human Rights Education, University of Leeds. She is studying the processes of introducing citizenship education, through action research in another London school where she was citizenship coordinator and which acted as a pilot for the introduction of citizenship education in England. Before teaching, Anne Hudson spent seven years working to support Namibia's struggle for independence. She has wide experience of working in partnership with teacher educators, examination boards and the Qualifications and Curriculum Authority to promote and support citizenship education.

Joe Lindsay is a BSc (Hons) Technology and Design student at the University of Ulster and a former pupil at Oakgrove Integrated College in Derry/ Londonderry.

Trevor Lindsay is a lecturer in social work at the University of Ulster in Derry. He worked for twenty years as a probation officer and manager in the West Yorkshire Probation Service, where he was a leading figure in antiracist probation practice and training. His research and publications focus on group work, probation practice, social work education and anti-sectarian social work practice. He is a governor of Oakgrove Integrated College, nominated by the Foyle Trust for its work in integrated education.

Roisin McLaughlin is director of the Northern Ireland democracy and social change programme at the UNESCO Centre, University of Ulster. She is a graduate of Auckland University in New Zealand, where she completed both a bachelor's and master's degree in political studies, with a focus on international relations, conflict intervention and human rights. She is currently completing a doctorate in education at Queens University, Belfast.

Ulrike Niens is research fellow at the UNESCO Centre, University of Ulster, where she is developing a research programme on citizenship education and democratic processes. Ulrike graduated in psychology at the Free University of Berlin and completed her PhD in social psychology at the University of Ulster. Her research interests and publications focus on peace education and conflict studies and address identity, reconciliation and social change.

Colm Ó Cuanacháin is secretary general of Amnesty International's Irish Section. He worked as principal of Ireland's first multi-denominational Irish language immersion primary school until 2000, when he became Chair of the International Executive Committee of Amnesty International. He completed his PhD at the Centre for Citizenship Studies in Education (CCSE) at the University of Leicester. Areas of academic interest include human rights education and citizenship studies.

Audrey Osler is Professor of Education and director of the Centre for Citizenship and Human Rights Education at the University of Leeds. She was formerly director of the Centre for Citizenship Studies in Education at the University of Leicester. She has worked as consultant in Europe, Africa and Asia for a number of organisations, including the Council of Europe, UNESCO and the Carter Center. She is diversity adviser to the Royal Air Force and was, from 2000-2003, a member of the British government panel on Sustainable Development Education. Her books include *The Education and Careers of Black Teachers* (1997); *Citizenship and Democracy in Schools* (2000); *Changing Citizenship* (2005, with Hugh Starkey); and *Girls and Exclusion* (with Kerry Vincent), winner of the 2003 TES/NASEN academic book award.

Jacqueline Reilly is research fellow at the UNESCO Centre, University of Ulster. She completed both her undergraduate degree and her doctoral research at the School of Psychology, Queen's University, Belfast. Her research activities and publications focus on the theme of social inclusion and diversity. She has been involved in a number of research projects relating to equality and, more specifically, to gender issues. Her research interests include the use of qualitative methodologies in social research.

Jill Rutter lectures in citizenship education at London Metropolitan University. She has worked on development projects overseas and taught geography in schools in London and Essex. From 1988-2001 she was education adviser at the Refugee Council. She is the author of *Supporting Refugees in 21st Century Britain* as well as 24 children's books. Her research interests focus on child migration and the reception of refugee children in countries of asylum and she has recently concluded research on the educational experiences and achievements of Congolese children in Britain.

Chris Wilkins is a former primary school teacher and is now lecturer in education and director of primary initial teacher education at the University of Leicester. His research interests lie within the field of citizenship education and the social contexts of education, with a particular focus on teacher training processes.

Citation Index

Index